Past Lives,
Present Dreams

Also by Denise Linn

A Pocketful of Dreams

Past Lives,
Present Dreams

HOW TO USE REINCARNATION
FOR PERSONAL GROWTH

DENISE LINN

PIATKUS

*This book is dedicated to my husband David
and my daughter Meadow . . .
fellow travellers through time and space*

This edition first published in 1994 by
Judy Piatkus (Publishers) Ltd
5 Windmill Street, London W1P 1HF

Reprinted 1995

This book is a new and expanded edition of the original version
of *Past Lives, Present Dreams* published in Australia in 1988

The moral right of the author has been asserted

Please note that *Past Lives, Present Dreams* reflects the personal
experience of the author. If you intend to follow any of the exercises or suggestions of the book, it might be helpful to do so
under the supervision of a therapist or other health care professional.

A catalogue record for this book is available from the
British Library

ISBN 0–7499–1377–0

Cover photograph by Johnny Rozsa

Set in 11½ on 12½ Ehrhardt by
Phoenix Photosetting, Lordswood, Chatham, Kent
Printed and bound in Great Britain by
Mackays of Chatham PLC, Chatham, Kent

*
Contents

*
Acknowledgements

Thank you, Leon Nacson, you are a true visionary.

Claire Brown, thank you for believing in me and my dreams.

Barb Kelly, it seems that we have known each other since the beginning of time. You are such a good friend.

Johnny Rozsa, you have made such a difference in so many lives.

Many thanks to Judy Piatkus, Gill Cormode and Anne Lawrance at Piatkus Books for guiding this book to completion.

To my Cherokee Uncle, Wade Scudder — though you are now with Great Spirit, I hear your whispers on the summer breeze and feel your kindness in the rising sun. I look forward to when we meet again 'on the other side of the river'. Wado!

*

Introduction:
The Time Is Now!

*I*t is an exciting time to be alive. There has never been a more powerful time to step beyond our personal limitations. There has never been a more potent time to step off the karmic treadmill into our full potential. It is only now, after aeons of evolutionary cycles, that each of us can come full circle into the blueprint of our own soul. The time is now! As we approach the end of the millennium we can finally resolve old issues that had their source in past lives and we can use our dreams to step into our true domain.

The seeds for this book about past lives and dreams were planted many years ago by my teacher, Dancing Feather of the Pueblo Indians. He was a humble man, yet he carried the great wisdom and power of his people within himself: 'He walked in beauty.' This loving man helped me to connect even more profoundly with my own Cherokee heritage as he shared prophecies for our time now and talked of the power of our dreams and the importance of releasing shadows from the past.

I remember being with him one warm summer evening as he sat cross-legged on the golden wild grasses of the sun-baked high mesa. This serene old medicine man was dressed in a faded cowboy shirt and well-worn jeans. A soft breeze rustled dried leaves, scattering them to either side of us. I strained to hear his gentle, low voice as he talked of the land and Mother Earth and Father Sky. His copper-coloured face seemed to glow as it reflected the crimson of the setting sun. His once jet-black hair was now a soft, peppered white. Deep lines of age were etched across his face, yet when he spoke he had an animated, child-like humility that seemed to transcend time. Sometimes when he was talking he would stop and stare into the distance. His eyes, clouded over with age, seemed to peer into some inner world for a moment. Then he would speak again.

He told me that Mother Earth was at the end of a long cycle and was about to renew herself. He said that we were at the time of completion and rebirth, and huge changes were going to occur in the fabric of our lives. The renewal would be difficult for many people because right now people were lost. They had lost their roots. They had lost the ability to be in 'right relationship' with all things. He said people didn't know who they were. They had forgotten how to find themselves in each and every part of nature. He said we were the mountains, the great sky, the meadows and the sea . . . we were all things great and small, but we had forgotten.

He talked of *the importance of our dreams* for nocturnal journeys as an entrance point to the inner realms. In the years ahead, he said, our dreams would be a valuable source of inspiration and healing, playing an increasingly important role in our collective evolution. He also explained that it was going to be essential in the years ahead to release the shadows of pain, suffering and old wounds from the past. The pain from the past was keeping us from experiencing fully the beauty around us. He said it was crucial that we learn to listen to our inner wisdom, and to the 'spirit ancestors' and guides around us. It was essential for people to 'reach for the stars' and remember who they were. He spoke with excitement about the great potential for us all in the time ahead.

As the years have passed since his death I have seen the wisdom of Dancing Feather's words. Our planet is indeed changing very quickly, just as he prophesied. As we face the end of the millennium, huge changes in technology and our natural resources are taking place. Our planet is changing so quickly that it is deeply affecting the way that we relate to each other and to our environment. We have 'forgotten' the primordial wisdom that all creatures and all things on our planet are connected. We have 'forgotten' that we are all connected within a living pulsating universe – a universe that is no less alive than the majestic whales in the sea or the wild flowers opening to the morning sun on the hillsides. We have 'forgotten' that we are living in a universe that sings with life, that pulses with intensity of spirit.

The universe is just as much alive as our human body. When we suffer injury to one part of ourselves, the entire body responds by sending healing energy to the site of the distress. We are not aware of the myriad biochemical processes that occur in our body's immune system. However, when we are injured our body responds automatically: it is a natural response. This is the nature of life . . . this is the nature of the universe.

The human body is a microcosm of the macrocosm of the universe. Our planet can be likened to one cell in the body of the living universe, and right now our planet is injured. The universe is sending healing energy to our wounded planet in the same way that the human immune system becomes activated when there is an injury to one part of the body. As wave after wave of healing energy infiltrates our planet, a massive purification is beginning to take place. There is a cosmic stirring up of old structures and institutions and limiting beliefs. Imagine a deep pond of stagnant water. The top six inches appears clear. But below the surface the pond is choked with silt and unhealthy growth. Suddenly a surging infusion of fresh, clear water from new springs below enters the stagnant pond. All the fetid water is churned up. The short-term effects seem chaotic and all is in turmoil. The pond looks worse – it appears muddy, decaying and foul. However, the purification is essential for the health of the pond, which soon becomes crystal-clear and sweet. Our planet now can be compared to that stagnant pond. The new frequencies that are being projected to the planet can be likened to fresh springs which cause upheaval but also create an incredible cleansing and clearing.

As we face the exciting and challenging times ahead we have enormous potential to release the heavy burdens we have carried from lifetime after lifetime. The cosmic stirring up of old structures and hierarchies means that struggles to overcome old blockages are currently surfacing. As new energies flood the planet, many people are experiencing an intense resurgence of old issues – resulting in temporary feelings of disorientation and upheaval. Many are having to deal with and resolve their grief and rage over old issues that previously had been suppressed or denied.

Denial of pain and suffering in this life, *as well as in previous lives*, is coming into the light now. Many people are struggling to overcome their barriers to wholeness. All the suffering, fear and pain of separation that have accrued lifetime after lifetime are now passionately yearning for absolution. This accumulation of thousands of years of lifetimes which exist inside of us, as suppressed memories, is now crying for release. It is only now that we have the opportunity to let go of old limitations from the past.

Deep within each of us is a vast interconnected inner universe. This inner universe is a realm where the past and present and future swirl in a great orchestration of light and sound. Right now, as we approach the end of the millennium, the veil between our personal inner universes and the outer universe around us is thinning. We now have the opportunity to step through our dreamtime portals into the mysterious realms of self, and become aware of inner truths that have been hidden from us for so long.

At the very heart of being, each individual has the opportunity to respond to an intuitive challenge of the heart. The challenge, in the years to come, is to be willing to face our shadow, to be willing to step through the veil of the night with courage and an open heart, to face who we have been in past lives so that we can live more richly in the present.

It is now time to be willing and ready to risk the journey into the darkest aspects of yourself ... to face your shadow. It is your shadow that separates you from Spirit. There are many shadows that present themselves in our lives – fear, pain, depression, sadness, self-limiting beliefs, disease and death. These shadows usually have their source in past lives. The journey beyond the shadows from the past, through the Veil of Illusion, does not need to take 'time', it only takes the willingness to risk. And only those who risk will truly live. Your inner journeys can be turning points in life and can bring about the deepest levels of transformation.

As the nocturnal door between the past, present and future is opening, your dreams can be used to reveal, and to heal the shadows of the past. By opening the portals to the dreamtime and healing your past lives you are prepared in the very depth of your being to face the coming challenges with grace and ease. Those who take that step beyond the illusion become master of their destiny and radiate a deep peace and joy to others. You can use your past life explorations and your dream journeys to move into the universal essence from which flow all life, all thought and all existence. In this oneness with all that is, you can unlock the deepest and the highest realities.

The process is the ancient and sacred journey of the soul in search of itself. Once you have chosen that path you may not return. However, it is a path that, once taken, will contribute to your experiencing powerful depths of love – love for self, love for others and for your planet. It is a path that allows you to connect with an energy that will contribute to your making a difference in the world.

*

ABOUT THIS BOOK

As the planetary changes increase, your past lives, your dreams and your inner guidance can be an increasing source of transformation and inspiration. But how can you best take advantage of the energies available at this time for growth and personal expansion? How can you 'remember' who you were in a past life? How can you release negative programming from past lives? What is a guide, and how can you contact your inner wisdom through your guides? How can you remember your dreams and how can you tell what your dreams are trying to tell you? Why is this such an important time in history? *Past Lives, Present Dreams* gives you simple, viable answers and solutions.

You *can* remember who you were in a past life. Anyone can. This book offers simple techniques to help you recall previously forgotten events from your past lives. It also explains reincarnation and karma, and why they are so important at this particular time in history. You can gain little-known information on how to use 'past life clues' to discover who you were in a past incarnation. You will discover how to use past life therapy to release persistent conditions that haven't responded to other types of therapy. You will come to understand how current fears and phobias, relationship difficulties, blockages to abundance and creativity, and physical ailments can be released using past life exploration. In *Past Lives, Present Dreams* you are told about specific techniques to resolve and release current difficulties that originated in the past.

Because of the current changes in the planet's energy fields, your spirit guides are much closer to your reality. They urgently want to 'speak' to you through your dreams and through your intuition. It is now becoming much easier to gain access to their wisdom for personal assistance in the important years ahead. In this book you can read about the different kinds of spirit guides and learn exercises which enable you to get in touch with your guides so that you can truly know what they are trying to tell you. And you can learn how to tell when your guides are near and how to 'tune in' to their wavelength.

As our planet's vibratory rate continues to accelerate it will be vital to listen to the messages within your dreams. For each dream carries secret messages from your soul that can assist you to stay in balance in the years ahead. Your dreams can assist the inner and outer healing that is taking place now. In this book you learn how to program, remember and interpret your dreams. In addition you learn how to use your dreams for past life explorations.

Throughout this book examples of past life regressions are used. Some of them are from clients with whom I have worked, others are from letters that were written after my past life seminars, and yet others are experiences that seminar participants shared with me. In some cases I have quoted the exact words from letters. Elsewhere I have paraphrased or shortened the description for easier reading. But I have always tried to be as close to the spirit of their experience as possible.

As we approach the beginning of a new millennium huge and exciting changes will occur on many levels within our multi-dimensional universe. There have been, and will continue to be, powerful shifts in the planetary vibratory rates. These changes have been foretold by native cultures around the world, and as they take place it will be exceedingly valuable to be able to find an oasis of inner peace within yourself. This can occur through releasing blockages and limitations from the past and through listening to your dreams and inner guidance. The aim of this book is to give you information and techniques to prepare you for the future. We are all the spiritual heirs of the planet, and the extent to which you can complete and release the past is the extent to which you can step into the future with love . . . and then there will be order and joy in the cosmos.

1

*

My Journey into Past Lives and Dreams

My own journey began very dramatically when I was seventeen, in the summer of 1967. I took my motorbike out for a ride on a country road in our small farming community in the American Midwest. It was a wonderful, warm, hazy, peaceful day. I felt so carefree as my hair blew in the wind. I flew past great fields of golden tasseled maize. Then, abruptly, my serenity was shattered.

A large blue car rammed into my motorbike from behind. The force threw me violently to the ground. I struggled to stand up. Shock turned to terror as I raised my head to look at my unknown assailant. With cold-blooded determination, he aimed a gun at me. The menacing, dark holes of the gun seemed enormous, out of proportion. My mind raced. Silent screams echoed in my brain. 'Why is this man aiming his gun at me? I haven't done anything to him! Why did he ram his car into my motorbike? I didn't do anything to him!'

Just before the deafening blast that changed my life forever, a thought ricocheted across my brain: 'He's aiming too low.' A split second later I was on the ground, shot down by a random killer who had already left a trail of murder in his wake. I was left on the side of the road, where a passing farmer found me and called an ambulance.

Everything seemed amplified. Harsh bright hospital lights. Sharp searing pain. Shrill voices. Slowly, the lights began to dim.

The pain subsided. I felt myself slip into a comfortable, soft black-ness. I was softly resting in a black, bubble-like cocoon. It was at this point, I was told later, that the doctors thought I had died.

Suddenly, the velvet-black bubble seemed to burst. I was bathed in a glorious, golden light. In fact, I wasn't just bathed in light – I *was* the light! I was all-pervading and luminescent. I then became aware of music which sounded unbelievably sweet and pure – ebbing and flowing sound waves of liquid light. That music was more beautiful than any symphony. This noble harmony pervaded my luminous spirit until I actually became the music. It seemed in that moment that I was made of noth-ing but magnificent, fluid light and sound. And the light and sound were not separate from each other, but merged together as one. And I was merged with the light/sound.

I had no sense of time. There was no past, no future. Every-thing was existing in the infinite present. I tried to think of the past, and couldn't. It was inconceivable, because it just didn't exist. It was as difficult to imagine linear time there as it is for me to experience non-linear time here. Everything just 'was'.

I was also overwhelmed with a deep, and very real, sense of familiarity. I knew I had been there before. It was the most real thing that I had ever experienced. It made my teenage life seem like an illusion – just a dream. It was like waking in the morn-ing after having a dream that seemed very real, and then, as the morning rolls by, feeling it fade away to wispy fragments. Like sparkling grains of sand flowing through my fingers, my life disappeared. The glorious realm I had entered was the only true reality. My previous life seemed nothing more than the passing murmur of the wind.

Infused in this abundance of light and sound and infinite 'now-ness' was a most perfect 'love'. How can I possibly com-municate to others what I felt? In each of us, at the very heart of our being, there resides an intuitive sense of love that is as natu-ral as breathing. It is a love beyond form, like a vast, unlimited ocean, penetrating every cell and molecule of our being. I had a deep inner awareness of this kind of love. It wasn't the type of love that you can fall into or out of. There was no separation – no 'me-ness' or 'you-ness' – in this love. It just 'was'.

And I wasn't alone. You were there too! In fact there wasn't anyone or anything that wasn't there. We were all there. Without bounds. Without separation. I was everyone. Everyone was me. I was everyone that I had ever helped. I was everyone that I had ever hurt. I was everyone that I had ever known. We were all one. Imagine a fantastic mirror ball in the sky. Radiating from it in all directions are shafts of light, creating myriad reflections that are spread throughout time and space. Imagine each person on earth identifying with one of the reflections. Now imagine each person identifying so very much with their own individual reflection that they forget we have all sprung from the same source. In fact we *are* the Source. A murderer's bullet had catapulted me beyond time and space. In that instance I remembered who I was and from where I had come. I returned to the Source. I felt a wonderful sense of deep peace and love and belonging. I no longer felt bound to my body . . . I experienced boundlessness. I felt a sense of unity with all of life. I had come home.

Although I felt that I had fused into oneness with all beings, I still had the ability to perceive from a fixed point of consciousness. From that centre point of awareness I noticed in front of me a great flowing river, emitting a soft golden light. As I looked to the far shore I knew that when I reached the other side I would never return to my seventeen-year-old body. I had never been happier. I would no longer have to bear the terrible pain of separation. I would no longer be trapped in a body ravaged by pain and suffering. As I took that first step into the river it didn't feel like water flowing around me. It felt more like an emergence into liquid light and sound.

I made my way halfway across the river. Fluid, shimmering, effervescent light parted on either side of me. But as I revelled in my homecoming, a voice, deep and ominous as an approaching storm, boomed, 'You may not stay here. There is something you still need to do.' I frantically resisted the order, screaming, 'Nooooooo!!!' But it felt as if I had been lassoed and was being dragged back to my physical body.

I woke up in a hospital bed, fighting for my life. Day after day I struggled not only with physical pain but with my tremendous grief about having to come back to my body. Every evening, however, I experienced a miracle. After the lights had been turned down and I was alone I would close my eyes. Then I would feel a hand gently slip into mine. A wonderful feeling of comfort and safety would flood my being. My eyes were closed when this happened, but sometimes I would open my eyes and look at my hand. Although I couldn't physically 'see' the hand that held mine, I could feel the contours of fingers and palm, and a radiating warmth. Sometimes during the night one hand would release mine and a different hand would fold lovingly into it. I particularly remember a very small, child-like hand comforting me one night. I knew I was safe. I knew I wasn't alone. I believe those hands belonged to angels.

The body into which I had been so reluctantly forced back was very damaged. The gunman's bullet had bounced off my spine, lodging in a lung and tearing away my spleen, an adrenal gland, and part of my stomach and intestines. Eventually one of my kidneys was removed and a plastic tube was inserted to replace the aorta from my heart. But in those few minutes something mysterious and magical had happened that altered the course of my life forever.

The doctors thought I would not survive because of the severity of my injuries. However, in the instant when I was thought to be dead, I went through a shift in consciousness that was responsible for my survival and rapid recovery. Although the shift was seemingly small, in its consequences it was enormous.

Imagine a river that is clogged with large, fallen trees and branches. To clear even a section of that river you would need heavy equipment as well as enormous effort and manpower. Now imagine that you follow the river to its source. You journey high on a silvery-thin trail to the topmost peak of a mountain range. At the summit of the mountain is a pure, clear spring with sweet, flowing water. As you reach down to remove a small stone you notice that the removal of the stone has caused the water to flow in a new direction. You have changed the course of the stream forever.

I feel that when I stepped into the golden light part of my

identity, like the small stone, was removed from my soul and changed the course of my life forever. This change of identity helped me to heal, because I experienced that I was more than my body. I knew I was Light and Spirit and Music and Energy and Love. The awareness made it much easier to heal my body. My body wasn't 'me'. My body was something that part of me inhabited, but I was so much more than my body. I had so many more resources to use to heal myself than just those available in my physical body.

*

A CHANGED LIFE

When I was beyond death's door, undergoing what I later discovered was called a 'near death experience', my identity of self shifted. This change in my perception of myself completely altered my life. It also contributed to my ability to heal myself, and in later years this shift of consciousness contributed to my ability to assist the healing of others.

Before I was shot I thought that 'I' was my body. Afterwards I saw the world entirely differently. I no longer thought that when my body died, I died. I no longer thought that my existence began at conception and ended at death. I no longer believed that I was separate from everything and everyone else on the planet. Time was no longer linear and staid. I no longer felt that the universe was governed by fixed, unchangeable rules of physics. The shift that occurred, when I was thought to be dead, changed forever my beliefs about the nature of reality.

Although the world around me looked physically the same, the context in which I experienced it was completely different. Life became very precious. Every moment was full of colour and form and sound and vibrant energy. Each blade of grass shimmered in its own light, singing its own song . . . a field of wild grasses was like a great orchestra of light and song. Trees had a deep, sonorous hum. Leaves unfurled to warm winds which felt like the breath of God. Each leaf seemed to chime with crystalline delicacy. Even the earth beneath my feet pulsed with the gentle cadence of life. I had great difficulty understanding how people couldn't feel and see the overwhelming beauty around them. I couldn't comprehend cruelty or violence. I knew that we were part of one huge, vibrant, living universe, and that we couldn't hurt another without hurting ourselves.

As a result of my near death experience I now believe that we are infinite and eternal, and that we are all intimately connected. Our 'cosmic shoelaces' are attached, so to speak. I can't truly get home until you do, and vice versa. I believe that time is malleable and changeable. I believe that you can change the past as well as the future. I believe in God and angels and guides. I believe that in this time/space continuum called earth we have all experienced past lives. I believe that our dreams can be a powerful source of inspiration and healing. I believe that we all have an innate ability to create and manifest the universe around us. I believe, in fact, that we are subconsciously creating it right now through our thoughts, feelings and the core beliefs that we have carried forward from other lifetimes.

Having a near death experience is the kind of event that moulds one's beliefs. Millions of people around the world have had experiences similar to mine, and certain elements are common to most of them. The initial stages of the experience usually involve a sense of deep peace, and either not feeling attached to the body or floating above it. Many people feel that they are being sucked into a tunnel with a light at the far end of it, and are greeted by Beings of Light or by people whom they have known but who have already died. In almost all cases they feel very loved and cared for. Often individuals have the opportunity to review their life from an observer's point of view. Almost always there is the notion that they haven't completed what they need to do on earth, but there is a tremendous reluctance to return to the body.

Research has shown that those who have had near death experience share some traits and in almost all cases are changed by the event. They tend to have less fear of death than most people. On the whole they experience a greater sense of inner peace, with a greater zest for living. In addition they are often drawn towards the caring professions. However, I don't think that I am special in having had a near death experience; in fact, I think I was so far off my spiritual path that it took a cosmic kick of that force to get me on my path. I believe that the universe is always whispering to each of us. If we don't listen to the whispers, we'll hear the screams. The day I was shot was like a huge shout from Spirit: 'Denise, remember who you are!'

That shout from Spirit continues to echo in my life. I have found that many of my conclusions about life have evolved since my near death experience. I came back 'knowing' that we are living in the most important time in the evolution of our planet. I now understand that what we each do, individually and collectively, with our consciousness is essential for the future of our planet. I developed a deep desire to understand life in the light of the past lives that we have lived, and I 'knew' that past lives can offer a key to open the door to deep personal healing. I 'knew' that we are never alone: there are always spirit guides and helpers around us, pouring out their love and wisdom. I also came back 'knowing' the immense potential available to each of us within our dreams. I 'knew' that dreams can be an avenue to travel back to Spirit. The rest of my life has been a quest to 'remember' who I am, and my explorations into past lives, guides and dreams have nudged me along that path.

✳

MY QUEST

Before I was shot I wanted to become a scientist, like other members of my family. However, after my near death experience that desire left me. Instead I wanted to discover why we are here and what our human destiny is. Eventually I went to a Zen Buddhist monastery, where I meditated in stillness for over two years. I didn't have any great enlightenment experiences, as I had hoped, but I did discover a lovely place of stillness inside me. This place is called 'the silence between thoughts'.

I also began to explore non-traditional healing. Conventional medical practitioners told me that, as a result of the severity of my injuries, I would be disabled for the rest of what would be only a short life. But I instinctively knew that I could heal my body without their kind of medicine. My spiritual journey towards health and healing led me to a Hawaiian kahuna or shaman. This woman, a great healer, agreed to train me only after discovering that I was of American Indian heritage. She opened the doors of my understanding so I could see, even more deeply, that Spirit resides in everything. She taught me how one can call upon Spirit in times of need. She showed me that life isn't always what it seems and that there is magic in the universe.

I believe that each person is guided to people and situations that will provide understanding and growth. I was also led to a remarkable Japanese woman called Hawayo Takata, a Grand Master of Reiki, which is a method of channelling healing energy from the universe. When we first met she announced that she had been waiting for me to contact her and enquired what had taken me so long! I ended up organizing some of her first courses for Westerners. Hawayo, who was not only my teacher but became a good friend, taught me to access the life force energy in such a way that it would surge down my arms for healing.

Each of my teachers helped me to insert a different piece of my life's puzzle as I began to discover my place in the universe. I also trained with an eccentric Shiatsu master. Through him I learned to balance the body through putting pressure on various points which are similar to those used in acupuncture.

*

DANCING FEATHER

Of all my teachers, the one who will always have a sacred place in my heart is Dancing Feather. I was with him as he lay dying in the Santa Fe Indian hospital, and remember being disheartened because he was slipping away so quickly. I felt a deep sense of loss and sadness because I was losing a good friend and teacher. I also felt a deep remorse that, in my apprenticeship with him, I hadn't taken the opportunity to learn more. I said, 'Dancing Feather. What is the most important thing that you would have me know?' With a gnarled brown finger he beckoned me to come closer. As I looked into his fathomless eyes it seemed as if I was falling into the stars. He softly whispered, 'Keep it simple', smiled and fell back on to his pillow. And slowly, like a gentle tide coming to shore, the truth of Dancing Feather's words sank in. I have never forgotten the wisdom of that statement. His very last words to me were, 'Wherever you are, wherever you go . . . I will be there.'

As I walked out of the hospital my heart was heavy, knowing that I would never see my dear teacher again in this life. I began to cry, at first slowly and softly. I looked overhead, where dark, formidable clouds were beginning to form. It had been a very dry year, and the crops were suffering from the lack of rain. Suddenly a cool wind began to blow. Then one huge drop after another began to bounce off the red, dusty earth beneath my feet. I began to cry harder. It began to rain harder. Ragged shafts of lightning tore across the sky. I felt that the Spirits of the Sky, too, were grieving for loss of my teacher. I began to run as pelting rain drenched the parched land. As I continued to run, my eyes blurred by the rain and my tears, I passed what I thought was an old drunk Indian slumped on the side of the road. As I went past him he flung his head up as if a steel bar had been pushed up his spine, looked straight at me and said, 'I won't forget.' Then he slumped forward again. I couldn't get over how much his eyes looked like Dancing Feather's eyes in that moment.

Dancing Feather was a man of few words, but when he did speak he always spoke the truth. 'Wherever you are, wherever you go . . . I will be there.' After his death a most peculiar thing began to happen. Whenever I conducted a seminar about healing, people who have the gift of 'seeing' would say, 'I see an Indian standing beside you.' And they would describe Dancing Feather. This surprised me, because at the time I hadn't mentioned my apprenticeship to anyone outside my immediate family. And then people began to tell me that feathers would appear for them at important junctures in their life. . . .

*

FEATHERS

One woman told me an unusual story – only one of so many such stories.

> I am a single mother with three young children. I was going through a very hard time in my life when I couldn't financially or emotionally take care of myself or my kids. I thought they would be better off without me. I arose one morning, having very clearly decided that I would commit suicide that day. I just couldn't go on another day. Just then I heard a knock at the door. I went to the door and looked to the left and right. There was no one there. Then, just as I was closing the door, I looked down. There at the doorstep, laid out perfectly, were three shiny, beautiful feathers. I looked at those feathers . . . and I thought of my three beautiful children and I knew that I was going to make it. Seeing those three feathers was a turning point for me. I am now financially and emotionally stable and really enjoying my life and my kids.

Again and again I heard stories about feathers appearing. Each feather seemed to have a message. Sometimes the message seemed to be, 'You're doing just fine. Keep going.' At other times they would apparently be indicating a direction to go in life. I believe the feathers are messages from Spirit. They are a fulfilment of the covenant that Dancing Feather made on his deathbed.

I believe that if you are reading this book feathers will begin to appear in *your* life. As you begin to discover who you have been in past lives, and as you begin to resolve old past life negative programming, feathers will begin to appear for you. By doing the exercises in this book you will have begun an incredible journey of self-exploration, and feathers will serve as reminders that you are not alone on your journey. There are spirit helpers around you right now, peering over your shoulder, loving you and guiding you. They are helping you 'remember' who you are by helping you release past blockages.

Whenever you see a feather, be still for a moment and listen to your inner voice. It can be a feather that you see on the ground or one that appears in your home or even one that floats down from the sky. It can be a little feather or a large feather. But each feather contains a message. Each feather is a messenger from Spirit. When you see that feather just stop wherever you are, even if it is only for a second. Listen. There is a message to accompany that feather. I share this gift from my teacher to you. He would have liked it that way.

✳

MY JOURNEY INTO HEALING, PAST LIVES AND DREAMS

Not only did getting shot set me on a spiritual quest to understand the inner nature of reincarnation, but immediately the door to my dreams flew open with great ferocity. Vivid and sometimes disturbing images flooded my being during the night. Sometimes these images seemed so real that the boundaries between waking hours and night hours were blurred. Sometimes my dreams were full of colours and sounds and smells, idyllic and even visionary in nature. Some of these dreams were profoundly soothing and reassuring, and I would even occasionally catch a fleeting glimpse of the place to which I had travelled when I was thought to be dead. I would clutch at these cloudy images, only to have them vanish like fine mist.

Often my dreams were disturbing. As those nocturnal doors of perception opened for me, I saw images that had been held back for a long time. Numerous images of past lifetimes, seemingly forgotten in the recesses of my mind, began to surge forward *en masse*. While in my dreams I experienced living in other times and places in history. Perhaps the onslaught of these images filling my night hours can be likened to a computer downloading information or to a dam whose walls have held back a great river for many years. Through my dreams I began to understand that so many of the beliefs I had about myself and the world came from experiences that I had had in other lifetimes. By experiencing these memories in my dreams I was bringing to consciousness old limiting beliefs, decisions and judgements that I had carried over lifetime after lifetime. Now I could begin to release them.

There is a psychological adage that says 'To relive is to relieve', and it seemed that these images surfacing in the night were helping me to 'relive' forgotten memories so that I could begin to 'relieve' the burden that the past was taking on my life. Using many techniques, including exploring my past lives in my dreams, I began to heal, physically and emotionally.

Healing

As I successfully healed myself from my terrible injuries, despite all odds, people came and asked if I might help them to heal as well. I began with hands-on healing. My practice developed very quickly and I began to work with numerous people, sharing the methods I had used for my own healing. I developed a natural ability to channel healing energy through my hands, and the results seemed remarkable.

When patients came to me for a treatment we began by first speaking very quietly together. I asked them what results they wanted for their treatment. This helped focus the direction of the treatment. I then asked him or her to lie flat on a massage table or a futon. Then I sat next to the patient and became very still. My breathing slowed down. I waited until I could feel a warm breeze of energy fill my body. My hands became very warm . . . almost hot. I began by placing my hands very softly on the patient's head until I felt the warm stream of energy within me begin to flow into them. I felt a continuous stream of light and sound and love flow through both of us.

Then I began pushing pressure points on the body; each point corresponded with a different organ or gland. As I massaged, I began to have powerful experiences, as though I was disappearing into the pressure point. Each point was like an immense tunnel to the stars, and I felt like I was falling through that tunnel into space. The 'patient' seemed to disappear. 'I' disappeared. There were only stars and light and harmonic sound. Each point had a different sound and a different colour. As I explored my patients' remarkable inner universes I saw that each point had a special harmonic or sub-frequency. I discovered that not only did each point connect with an infinity of inner universes, but in fact there was a direct connection between each point and a specific location, power point or vortex on the earth, as well as with a specific point in the universe.

Each point that I pushed not only balanced the organs and glands of the physical body while it assisted the release of negative emotions, but also reached into the innermost and outermost places of their being. I 'knew' that in the still quietness of my healing room the world was a better place because of what we were doing. Healing energy was radiating from each pressure point on the human body to each power point on the planet . . . and each power point in the universe.

Each point seemed like an echo heard throughout the universe. Each point synchronised both healer and patient with the primordial rhythm of the farthest reaches of the galaxy. In those healing sessions I felt very close to connecting to the infinite light and love that I had felt in my near death experience.

And, apparently miraculously, with each treatment not only did my patients greatly benefit but I was being healed as well. Both healer and patient entered into an exquisite realm of love and healing. I believe that some of the most powerful healing comes when you can step beyond the bounds of separation. It comes when you are no longer healing someone who is separate from you. You enter into an exquisite place where the bounds of separation diminish. You are no longer the healer, nor are they the patient. You are both engaged in a cosmic dance through the stars.

I also began to realize that all the healing I was doing on others was essentially 'self-healing'. I discovered that each patient I worked with was a part of my greater 'self' that dwells in all people and in all things. Each of my patients was a different aspect of the greater 'me', and represented a particular part of my 'self' that needed help.

For example, at one stage a number of cancer patients came for treatment. As I worked with them I realized that there were a number of similarities between us. Their cancer was eating away at them and, though I didn't physically have cancer, I had some emotional issues that were 'eating away' at me. The things that were 'eating away at me' seemed to be spontaneously transformed at the same time as my patients were experiencing positive results with their sessions. I realized that the healing process always began with me. 'I' was never healing anyone else but my 'self'.

In my hands-on healing practice I usually had excellent results. Every once and a while, however, I would work with someone whose physical or emotional pain would leave – only to return later. This was frustrating to me. Realizing that many of our current problems have their source in the past, I began to regress patients to earlier incidents in their lives – often back into their early childhood.

Past Lives

I often used relaxation techniques for my regressions. I would ask my patients to lie down and relax, helping them with breathing techniques and visualization processes. I would then suggest remembering an incident from the previous day. After my patient had relived this memory I would then suggest going back to a memory from the previous week. After that I would continue taking them back in time until they arrived at early childhood. In this way my patients were able to retrieve previously forgotten memories and heal old emotional wounds. I found that many present-day problems were healed by regressing to early childhood and releasing early negative decisions and beliefs.

For example, a man with a very sore shoulder came to me for

hands-on treatment. After I had worked on him, the shoulder was fine. However, three weeks later the pain returned. I then helped the man regress to a time when, as a young boy, his father had struck him on the shoulder. The father felt that his son wasn't meeting his responsibilities, and had hit him. Now, as a grown man, he felt he wasn't being responsible enough. He associated feeling irresponsible with having pain in his shoulder. So any time he felt irresponsible he recreated the sore shoulder.

We subconsciously recreate situations in the present that are similar to our circumstances in the past. We do this as a way of re-stimulating the repressed emotions from the past, so that we can release them. When my patient regressed to his childhood, he was able to experience the grief and pain and feeling of unfairness that he had suppressed at the time his father struck him. By releasing those emotions, he was able to ease the pain in his shoulder. As young children we all make decisions and judgements that are still influencing our present lives. I discovered that helping someone regress back to the time in his life when vital negative decisions were made could, more often than not, release those decisions and the corresponding symptoms *forever*.

However, there were a few persistent cases where, even after a regression to childhood, the symptoms returned. I was very puzzled by this. Janet had suffered from ulcers for years. She was in the hands of a traditional doctor who had prescribed drugs. She had also changed her diet and, at her doctor's suggestion, enrolled in stress reduction classes. However, the ulcers persisted and she intuitively felt there was something else she could do that would help. She came to me for a treatment, and we decided that we might find some clues to her condition in her early childhood. She regressed to the age of twelve, then ten, seven, six . . . and suddenly she became very distressed. Her breathing increased sharply and she began to hyperventilate. I told her she could watch the circumstances around her calmly, and asked what she was experiencing.

'I've been poisoned!' she said.

I said, 'When you were six you had some poison?'

'No! I've been poisoned!'

I was concerned, thinking that we had uncovered a memory where as a young child she had been given poison. I asked, 'Who is poisoning you?'

She answered, 'Enemies of my husband are forcing me to take poison.'

I knew she wasn't married, so momentarily I was confused. 'Where are you?' I asked.

'I'm in India.'

I asked her to describe what was happening. Janet proceeded to tell me she was the young wife of an older husband who had very strong political beliefs, in opposition to those who were in power. She described the anguish she experienced. Though she loved her husband and wanted to support him, at the same time she didn't like the disharmony that his beliefs were causing in their life. One night, when her husband was away, his enemies broke into her house and forced her to drink poison. She died feeling helpless and powerless.

I asked her to go back in time into the life that she was seeing and 'replay' it, making some decisions that would make her feel less helpless and more in charge of her life and her destiny. She did so, and saw herself actively campaigning to get other people in the village to understand her husband's point of view. She saw other people rallying around her husband so that he had a strong platform of support which provided strength and protection. She 'saw' that she and her husband raised a family and each died at a ripe old age, well loved in the community. As she explained this revised scene to me, her entire countenence changed and her face shone with a deep peace.

After this session we talked about her present life. She was in a relationship where she felt helpless. She said that the ulcers had started about the same time that she entered into it. We talked about some choices she could make in her present relationship. Within a few weeks the ulcers had completely healed, and they didn't return.

In Janet's current life her relationship difficulties had activated early similar memories from a past life. In her subconscious she had equated feeling helpless with poison eating holes in her stomach. When she felt helpless in her current life this activated the past life physical trauma, and so she got an ulcer which ate holes in her stomach. During our session she had activated a subconscious memory of being poisoned at a time when she was feeling helpless in a relationship. By changing the images in her subconscious she was able to change negative programming that was affecting her present life.

When I saw the results in Janet's life I was very excited by the potential of regression into past lives. Dealing with problems only in present time can be likened to mowing dandelions. You can mow them down, but they will keep surfacing again and again. It is only when you dig down to the roots that they won't resurface. In my therapy practice, when I found a problem that couldn't be solved by exploring early childhood, I would regress the patient to the 'roots' of the problem in a past life. After resolving the past life issues, their symptoms would almost always disappear permanently.

I found that most of our present blockages can be traced back to a past life. By going back and experiencing what had occurred in the past we can heal physical and emotional challenges. With past life therapy my patients released ailments and phobias. They mended relationship difficulties, increased their creativity and released blockages to abundance. The results were amazing.

Later, I discovered another technique for tuning into past lives. When I pushed with my thumbs on a Shiatsu point in my hands-on healing, often I would see images in my mind. In addition, the person I was working on would often spontaneously see the same images in their mind. Sometimes these were images from their early childhood that they had forgotten, but more often they would be images of past lives.

I began to realize that past life memories are not only lodged in our brain but are also lodged in the body, and stimulating those images for recall had enormous positive results in my patients' lives. I realized that every cell in our body has consciousness, and that each cell lodges emotions and past life memories. Just as DNA/RNA has encoded into its structure a blueprint for our physical body, I believe that within its intricate structure there are memories for this life and past lives! This was an important discovery for the work that I was later to do with group past life regressions, when I got people to stimulate points on the body to help facilitate past life recall.

Many of my clients began to report that after my treatments their dreams began to change, to feature images and memories of other times in history. It seemed that, once the doors to the past opened, dreams were used as a processing point to release the accumulation of thousands of years of lifetimes that were longing for release.

I was so excited about my clients' results that I began to use past life regressions in my personal life. At the time I had a weight problem. I was one of those individuals who was constantly dieting – losing the weight and then putting it back on again. I weighed over 170 pounds. I could lose about 10 pounds, but I would inevitably gain it back again. When I discovered the power of regression, I regressed myself to a time in my childhood. There I 'saw' an image of myself as a three-year-old being told by my mother what a big girl I was. It was her way of letting me know that I met with her approval. For some reason, this had a very dramatic effect on me. I equated 'big' with 'good'. Later, as an adult, I naturally wanted to be 'good', so I was subconsciously helping my body to get 'big'. Once I had made that realization, I lost 15 pounds without even trying. But I still didn't weigh what I felt was ideal for me. I kept struggling to meet my weight goal, but without success. At this point, I once more had a startling revelation within a dream.

My dream was very vivid. Dust assailed my nostrils. Billows of golden clouds of dust surrounded the buffalo herd as it stampeded by. Upwind, my nostrils were sensitive to the fetid odour of the fear-smeared beasts. I felt rooted to the land and, strangely, the buffalo charge seemed to reflect the restless stirrings in my soul. Waking up from this dramatic dream, I knew that in my night hours I had been transported over the bridge of time to a past life as an American Indian woman. The images and smells in the dream were very real, the shimmering colours very alive. In my waking hours I used my dream as a starting point to regress to a past life where I recalled being a member of a wandering Blackfoot tribe. After having the dream, images and feelings began to fill me spontaneously – even, unexpectedly, during my waking hours. I began to see how many of the habits in my current life could be traced back to that Blackfoot life.

We were a nomadic tribe who had to keep moving to find enough to eat. In the winter there wasn't always enough food. Even when there was enough food, there was an eating hierarchy. The male elders ate first, then the chiefs and warriors, and finally the young women and children. As an old, physically impaired woman I was often the last to eat and would go to sleep hungry.

I saw how this experience in a past life had set in motion a pattern in my present life. At mealtimes, in my present life, whenever there was a communal dish rather than individual servings I felt an intense panic fill me. I was afraid that I wasn't going to get enough to eat. Whenever I was served I would eat voraciously, even if I wasn't hungry. This created physical problems, since I ate so fast that the food wasn't being digested properly, and I was also eating more than my body needed. In those moments of panic I was re-enacting my memories of not having enough to eat. Experiencing my relationship to food as a Blackfoot Indian helped me understand my present relationship to food. As I released the belief that I wasn't going to get enough food I was able to slow down when I ate, and to start eating more in accordance with my body's needs rather than out of an old fear about survival.

In my life as an old Indian woman I developed a hip problem that prevented me from keeping up with the tribe during their moves between camps. It was a tribal tradition to leave the old people behind when they could not keep up. Consciously, as an Indian woman, I understood this: I knew it was necessary to leave the old behind to ensure that the rest of the tribe survived. However, subconsciously in that life I experienced anguish, loneliness and the bitterness of betrayal. These feelings were at odds with my acceptance of the ways of the tribe. My emotions became confused and suppressed.

The images and feelings from my life as a Blackfoot are very clear. After I was abandoned, I remember finding shelter in a small indentation of rock – not quite a cave. The walls feel rough and cold to my touch. The late autumn air is harsh and cold. Each breath of air bites sharply inside my nostrils and creates an icy burn inside my lungs. The cold rips through my clothes, rips through my thoughts, rips through the last vestige of warmth left me. The sky is a pea green-grey. The snows are late, so there isn't even the comfort of soft blanketing whiteness to assuage the stark reality of being abandoned. The far black mountains are ragged against the sky. Barren branches are silhouetted against a greasy grey horizon, punctuating my aching loneliness. It's bitterly cold. My hand are frozen. I can't feel my feet. Hunger eats away at my reason. 'How could they leave me! I thought that they were my friends. I worked so hard. I gave so much. How could they leave me. I give up. Let me sleep. Let me die. Let me die. Let me die. . . .'

I starved and froze to death with feelings of extreme resentment and loneliness. The feelings and decisions that we have at death are very powerful and often carry forward lifetime after lifetime. It's not all the emotions that carry forward. It's the suppressed emotions and feelings – what we didn't allow ourselves to experience and express at the time – that create present day blockages.

So starving to death didn't create the blockage that resulted in my overweight body – it was the emotions that I suppressed that had carried into my current life. Recalling that Indian memory, I was able to understand why, every time I had tried to diet to lose weight in this life, I would feel incredibly lonely and back away from the emotional pain. I subconsciously equated a lack of food with memories of being abandoned and lonely. When I allowed myself to experience those painful emotions I had suppressed in that former life, I lost the remaining pounds I wanted to lose! Furthermore, I have found that past life therapy is an excellent adjunct to any weight loss program for anyone interested in keeping the pounds off. Some 95 per cent of people who lose weight through dieting put it back on again. Those who lose weight by going to the emotional source of the problem, which is often in a past life, are usually able to keep it off for good.

Discovering my past life as a Blackfoot Indian also enabled me to unravel mysteries that were creating barriers in my present life. Whenever we moved we were required to carry heavy things over long distances. In my present life I was always carrying heavy things, often when I didn't need to. Sometimes I would even pick up a heavy stone and carry it for a long distance, for no reason. Not only was this a peculiar habit, but it was also damaging my spine. As soon as I recognized where this pattern came from I no longer felt any compulsion to carry heavy things.

In my life as a Blackfoot woman I was a healer, administering herbs, attending births and soothing wounds (all things that I have done in this life). Although I was an excellent healer of others, my hip problem made me feel unworthy of marriage as I seemed to equate physical ability with worthiness. I never married in that life. I also blamed the tribe, and thought it was the tribe that saw me as unworthy.

Transported into that life as an American Indian, I realized that it was not the tribe's judgement, but my own self-judgement, that made me turn suitors away. In my present life, from early childhood I had assumed that I would never marry. Later, the injuries sustained at the time of the shooting made me feel undesirable as a women, further promoting the idea that I would never marry. Travelling back in time to that point where I had made the initial decision as an Indian woman, and reliving it, seemed magically to lift my lifelong blockage to having a fulfilling relationship. I now have a wonderful husband, whom I call the man of my dreams.

So many things in my present life shifted once the door to that particular Blackfoot life opened. I had always suffered from poor circulation in my feet and hands, even in a warm climate such as that of Hawaii. This was a legacy from my freezing to death as an Indian. I also found that, whenever I got cold, I felt isolated and emotionally numb. I never could understand winter sports and skiing. It didn't make sense to me that people would choose to be cold on purpose!

Just changing the decisions I had made in that past life made such a difference in my twentieth-century life. Afterwards my circulation improved so much that it is much better than most people's. And now I love winter sports. In fact, cross-country skiing is probably about as close as I come to connecting with God. I love the pure white blanket of snow. I love the stillness of a snow-shrouded forest. I love to watch the soft crystals float from a high branch overhead when a gentle breeze shakes the tree. I love the swishing cadence of the skis as they glide effortlessly through the sparkling snow. All this joy would have eluded me if I had not explored my past life.

Another old pattern began to dissolve after seeing my Indian past life. I always needed to be included in group activities, and I was always trying to get everyone to like me, even if it meant denying what I knew intuitively to be right according to my intuition. I was voted 'nicest' girl in high school, which at the time seemed a wonderful honour. Later I recognized what it meant: that I had had to give up so much of my own truth to get everyone to like me. In my subconscious was a core belief that if people liked me I would survive. When I was dying as an old Indian woman I kept thinking that, if my fellow tribal members had liked me more, perhaps I wouldn't have been left behind. So I came into this life thinking I had to get everyone's acceptance. The inner recognition that I didn't have to attain everyone's approval freed me to find my truth. I could act on my truth and 'be' my truth. This created an enormous shift in my life.

Each past life contains seeds that sprout in our current life. Dying cold and hungry while feeling betrayed created an emotional charge on betrayal. In my current life I had created situation after situation in which I felt betrayed. In each of these situations I became a whirlpool of emotions – rage, bitterness, resentment, sadness and grief. In every situation in which I felt betrayed I would find out later that I had actually not been betrayed. This was the exact pattern of the events that occurred to me as an Indian. I wasn't betrayed. I knew that if I couldn't keep up I would be left. I knew this was a tribal law, and moreover one that I adhered to. I wasn't actually betrayed, but I felt that I was. We keep recreating the same patterns over and over again until we release them from our personal energy field. I don't create instances where I feel betrayed any more. And if I ever did, I feel that I would now be an observer, watching an old pattern unfold rather than being cinched into the death throes of the feelings and emotions which used to surround the event.

After my past life exploration into my life as an Indian woman, I understand my interest in herbs. I have owned a herb company in this life and often use herbs for healing. I also understood my deep love of nature. I realized why I collected antlers. To an Indian, antlers had many uses including that of tools. Subconsciously I can still feel the value of these beautiful creations. I understood my love for the drum and drum rituals. I can trace so many of my present views of life back to my existence as a Blackfoot. Currently I lead Indian ritual sessions such as medicine wheel ceremonies, vision quests, and sweat lodges, as well as teaching drumming, and drum making and painting. All of this gives me great joy. I have pulled forth what was beautiful and sacred from that past life and incorporated it into my present life. Not only is it valuable to release limiting patterns from the past, but you can also pull out talents and abilities from that time.

I have Indian blood in this life, and I was an Indian in a past life. In my past life therapy with patients I find that our present-day heritage can often give clues about a past life. In the past I found that being an Indian was a hard and difficult life. In my present life I am proud of being Native American. This honouring of my heritage helps heal the difficulty I had in the past.

I also experienced another past life that was dramatically influencing my present life. For most of my adult life I had struggled with finances and possessions. As soon as I received any money or was given any material object, I seemed to find a good reason for giving it away. I had an incessant need to be without possessions and money. Another aspect of this was my choice of clothing. I was inclined to wear the same style of clothing day in and day out, and was reluctant to buy anything new. When I discovered that in one past life I had been a Franciscan monk on a small island off Venice, I was able to understand why I had difficulty creating abundance in this life. I 'saw' this life during an experience of déjà vu when I visited this island monastery.

I remembered my life as a monk. I remembered the radiant morning sun pouring through my monastery window. The birds seemed to be chirping a canticle to the cosmos. What a glorious day to be alive! In fact, every day was glorious in the praise of the Lord. My small cell filled with the approaching warmth of the day. I placed my feet on the stone floor. The stones still held some of the coolness of the night and felt smooth and comforting to my bare feet. After my most earnest prayers, though my heart was bursting to run, I maintained a restrained decorum in front of the elder brothers as I walked to the garden. I loved working in the garden. The richness of the soil in my hands filled me with contentment and peace. The sound of the birds overhead was like the greatest chorus of angels to my ears. A small tendril reaching forth from a dark black seed that I had planted was a most wondrous event to me. My life was simple, yet filled with a deep, rich peace. I had strong feelings about right and wrong. Money and possessions were wrong. Poverty was good. Poor people were God's chosen. Anyone who broke any of the commandments was wrong.

Anything that you judge as right or wrong cleaves itself to you lifetime after lifetime. In that past life, I had taken very powerful vows of poverty and decided that possessions were wrong. In my present life, whenever I was given a present I began to feel uncomfortable and anxious and felt a compulsion to give it away. All material possessions filled me with the same anxiety. The subconscious memories of these vows and of my life as a monk were influencing my present life to the point where I couldn't allow myself any possessions.

The energy from my past life as a monk was very strong within my current life. As well as those two years in a Zen monastery I spent long periods of time in solitude and retreat. Even when I wasn't living in a monastery, I used to wear the same style of clothing as the Franciscan monks. Every day I would put on a long brown tunic of rough woven cotton over rough brown pants, and large sandals. I wore this outfit to work, at home – even to weddings and other special events. By releasing the vow that I made as a Franciscan, I acquired more freedom and abundance in my present life.

I realized that material things are not themselves bad – it is our attachment to or identification with material objects that can create difficulty. After releasing my vows of poverty I could be more free to choose what I wanted to have in my life and what I didn't want. I was no longer being controlled by a past decision. I could decide if I wanted to have possessions or not, and do so without feeling guilty. The vows that we make in this life and in past lives have an enormous affect on us. It is valuable to recognize and release any limiting vows from past lives that may have a hold on you.

Group Regressions

I was so encouraged by my clients' results and those that I was seeing in my own life that I did not hesitate to accept an offer to teach a course about past lives. I began to do group regressions in these courses and was amazed to see that the same, if not better, results could be produced with large groups of people. I began working with between one hundred and nine hundred people at a time, usually averaging around two hundred. I began to notice that over and over again in these large groups many people would experience past lives in the same country and same period in history. It was as if they had subconsciously decided to come together once again at this exciting juncture to release not only individual karma but collective group karma as well. This idea is based on the theory that you incarnate lifetime after lifetime with other like-minded individuals. These souls can be compared with a flock of birds that migrates to distant countries, yet always flies together. Information gathered in my reincarnation seminars has consistently shown that individuals incarnate in groups and tend to be drawn together again and again, lifetime after lifetime.

A striking example occurred in Canberra, Australia a number of years ago. I had been invited to present a past life seminar which included a regression meditation. During past life meditations I don't give any clues that might presuppose someone towards a particular past life or towards a particular time in history. I only will say something like 'You are standing in the mists of time, and when the mists lift you will be in one of your past lives.' After the past life process I took a show of hands. It indicated that over two-thirds of the hundred people in the room felt that, during the regression, they had experienced a past life in Rome! Rome was never mentioned before the process, so they weren't pre-programmed to think of this kind of life. On examination, it seemed plausible that those individuals who in a past life had lived in ancient Rome (a planned city that was the centre for government, peopled by many government employees) would have chosen to incarnate in Canberra (another planned city that is a centre for government, peopled by many government employees).

At a past life seminar in Seattle there were an inordinate number of people who said that they had been World War II fighter pilots; at another seminar a large number said that they had been American Pilgrims, and at yet another many were American Indians. I don't feel that these are coincidences; I believe that, long before this current life, the participants at each seminar made a choice to come together again, as a group, to release limitations from shared past lives.

I received a letter recently from a woman in Germany who had attended a past life workshop that I had presented in Australia. She was writing to tell me of a remarkable experience that she had had at this time. During the seminar I play music and then ask the participants to walk round the room. I tell them that when the music stops they may very well be standing next to someone whom they knew in a past life. Most people, of course, think this is rather ridiculous but do the exercise anyway. Ursula wrote to say that when the music stopped she was 'coincidentally' standing next to another German. There were over two hundred people in the seminar and she hadn't seen him before. As they talked, they found that they had been born in the same small German village! While she was growing up she had walked past his house every day on her way to school. They had each moved to Canada, to the same town, at approximately the same time – and they had both moved to the same town in Australia at the same time. Now this could be an amazing coincidence, or it could lend credence to the idea that we are attracted to each other again and again lifetime after lifetime. This letter is not unusual: I have received hundreds of similar ones from people who have attended my reincarnation workshops.

Sometimes at the end of a session I'll ask if there is anyone who wants to describe what they 'saw' during their past life meditation. At a London seminar a man stood up and said he saw that he was an American Indian standing by a cliff; then another Indian came and pushed him over the edge. When he had said this, the man sitting next to him (whom he didn't know) went very pale. I asked this man, 'What did *you* experience during the past life process?' He answered in a quavery voice, 'I was an American Indian and I was pushing someone off a cliff!' On another occasion a woman said that she remembered a life in nineteenth-century London where she was in a public park pushing someone in an old wooden wheelchair. The women next to her looked startled and said in her meditation she had 'recalled' a life in nineteenth-century London where she was in a public park and being pushed in a wheelchair. One man relived a life in which, as a native of the Amazon jungle, he had helped to destroy an entire neighbouring village. The person sitting next to him (a stranger) had experienced watching his entire village in the Amazon being wiped out by a neighbouring tribe.

I found that in large groups a tremendous energy can be generated that makes it easier for past life exploration and personal healing. Whenever possible I place healers and therapists around the edge of the room during the past life regressions, generating healing energy and a heart space (a place of love) so that people's experiences are positive, empowering and healing. I am now teaching traditional therapists how to incorporate past life regression techniques into their work. The expansion of interest in reincarnation by the Western world gives credence to the idea that, as we catapult into the future, there is a collective need to understand where we have come from so that we are better prepared for what lies ahead.

You can dynamically change your life forever using the very simple reincarnation techniques described in this book. You don't need to go to a therapist or a past life seminar – you can begin your exploration in your own home right now. The increasing intensity of the planet's vibaratory rate has made it much easier to be aware of your past lives. Just reading this book, even if you don't do any of the exercises mentioned, may begin to help you to heal negative programming from your past lives. As you put your awareness on resolving your past lives you may notice your dreams beginning to change. Watch your dreams. Also, begin to observe the patterns and circumstances of your life. Many people will begin to activate past life patterns just through reading this book. As these patterns are being activated, you can begin to heal the past using the methods described in this book. There has never been a more exciting time to be alive. There has never been a more powerful time to resolve old issues and old negative programming. Life *is* a great and grand adventure.

2

*

Reincarnation
and
Karma

*T*he concept of reincarnation, the central focus of past life therapy, has been around since before recorded history. Over a third of the people alive today believe in it. The basic idea is that the soul is eternal and returns to earth again and again, through rebirth into new bodies, in order to grow and learn. Each lifetime provides a wealth of experiences that allow each of us as Spiritual beings to become stronger, more balanced and more loving, and eventually to reunite with Spirit. I prefer to use the word 'Spirit' instead of 'God' because some people equate the word God with a male, judgemental deity in the sky. To me God, Great Spirit, Spirit, Cosmic Consciousness all define the same thing, which is the Living Force within all things.

Have you ever had the eerie experience of being in a strange town and feeling a familiarity almost too deep to describe? Have you heard a particular piece of music and felt transported by it? Or have you ever had a vivid dream about a time in history or a foreign country that seemed extraordinarily familiar and real? All these incidents can have their roots in other lifetimes.

In one life, perhaps a soul might be very poor and thus have a chance to learn humility and resourcefulness. In another, it might be wealthy in order to learn about dealing with money fairly and positively. It might be blind, in order to learn inner sight, or athletic, in order to experience and understand physical strength. A soul might be a woman in one life and a man in another, or of white Caucasian stock in one and Asian in another. You could think of past lives not so much as building blocks but as pieces of a jigsaw puzzle with each piece (lifetime) making us more complete and balanced.

*

REINCARNATION AND HISTORY

Throughout history, great thinkers have pondered the mysteries of life, birth and rebirth. The earliest record of reincarnation comes from ancient Egypt. It says that the soul is immortal and that when the body perishes the soul enters into another human body. The ancient and present-day Hindus are another example of a group of people who believe that the soul is immortal and inhabits one body after another in its search for its true divine nature. Centuries before Christ, Buddha taught about the cycle of reincarnation – the great wheel of life and death. Buddhists, like Hindus, strive to be released from the death/rebirth cycle by attaining nirvana or oneness with God. The Essenes, an early Jewish sect, are also said to have believed in reincarnation.

The Greek philosopher Pythagoras, who lived some five centuries BC, not only spoke of reincarnation in his writings but described his personal recollections of his various incarnations. His fellow philosopher Plato was also a believer. Napoleon said he had been the eighth-century Holy Roman Emperor Charlemagne in a past life. The French philosopher Voltaire, observed that 'It is not more surprising to be born twice than once.' The Spanish surrealist painter Salvador Dali said he believed he was the great Spanish mystic St John of the Cross. And famous Americans including Benjamin Franklin, Henry Ford and Thomas Edison all believed in reincarnation.

The idea of reincarnation becoming a viable personal philosophy is becoming more prevalent in Western cultures. Many people nowadays find that their spiritual needs aren't being met by current religions or philosophies, and are turning instead to the understanding of reincarnation. It answers questions such as why we keep repeating the same negative patterns again and again; where our recurring fears and phobias come from; why we feel an instant attraction to some people and some places; and, more importantly, what our purpose is here on earth. The philosophy of reincarnation allows us to understand what determines how we each weave our own destiny.

*

SOULMATES

One of the most important areas that reincarnation philosophy addresses is the understanding of relationships. Understanding and healing relationship difficulties, most of which have their roots in past lives, can help re-establish the quality of relationships in present life. The latter, which are our karmic counterparts, give us the chance to complete any unfinished task and help us to release negative thoughts and negative emotions that may intrude into this lifetime. People with whom we had relationships that originated in a past life are called soulmates.

Have you ever had a brief encounter that left such a searing impression of intensity that you could never quite shake off the memory? Although it was years ago, I can clearly remember queuing for a film when a tall, serene man emerged from the darkness and walked past. My breathing stopped. My knees went weak. I had to grab the side of the building to stop myself from fainting. When I turned to look at him, he was gone. Who was this man to whom I had such an extraordinary response? A psychologist might say that I had activated a hidden memory from my childhood of someone who looked similar to that tall stranger. However, it's very likely that the object of my fleeting glance was a soulmate.

How many times have you briefly caught a glimpse of someone across a crowded room and felt an instant rapport, an inner knowingness of a kindred spirit. In one brief moment, did you feel a yearning to rekindle those memories from the past and hold on to them for an eternity? Or, alternatively, have you ever met someone and instantly felt uncomfortable, confused and perhaps even angry?

These meetings are all part of a complex web of intrigue that lies deep within our subconscious minds, and tapestries of events weave their way throughout each of our lifetimes. This determines the way we interact with those around us. They may cause us to feel a deep love or desire for one individual – or hateful, envious or spiteful to another. The soul memories are roused and relationships are rekindled. Almost everyone with whom we connect in this life is likely to have been involved in many of our past lives, perhaps as a brother, sister, colleague, child, lover or parent.

Many of the effects of those past life experiences are created again in this life. They may perhaps be passionate and romantic, adventurous, or steeped in revenge, envy and hatred. It is at this junction that we meet again to relive and rework the relationship. Those familiar eyes across a crowded room are a soul reminder of the individuals with whom we have chosen to interact once again, and the encounter provides us with the opportunity to deal with those karmic relationships.

The idea of a soulmate usually evokes images of Romeo and Juliet, Tristan and Isolde or Katharine Hepburn and Spencer Tracy – images of a most exquisite love that seems to transcend time and space, with two people finding their perfect complement in each other. Though the term 'soulmate' is commonly used to describe the one great love of your life, I believe that soulmates can be defined as *all* those individuals whom you have been with time after time after time in past lives and even in other dimensions. This idea is based on the theory that you incarnate lifetime after lifetime with other like-minded individuals. Soulmates tend to incarnate together and are attracted to each other even in the far reaches of the world.

A personal example of how soulmates are attracted to each other occurred for me as a young university student in the Midwest. I had been very much in love with a professor there and we shared a small country home. Sensing that he was seeing another woman, I became distraught, packed my bags and moved to Hawaii to put the soured love affair behind me. Some time later I moved to a new address in Hawaii, in the university district. Over tea with a friendly neighbour we discovered that we had both gone to the same large university. We even knew some of the same people. As she began talking about a clandestine affair she had had with a college professor, the truth slowly dawned upon me – I was speaking to my previously unknown Nemesis. She was the woman with whom my lover had had an affair. Luckily the situation was far enough behind us that we could become good friends.

There is a tendency to think that our soulmates are only those individuals whom we meet and with whom we feel an instant affinity. However, I have found in my regression work that soulmates can also be those individuals with whom we experience difficulties in our present lives. In fact, such challenging individuals are often those with whom we have had the most intimate past life connections.

When soulmates meet there is usually instant rapport or recognition, or even repulsion. If there has been a sexual liaison in a past life there will be a tendency for a physical attraction to occur in the present life, sometimes almost explosively intense. Although soulmates don't always see eye to eye, a sense of familiarity usually accompanies the relationship. It is a communication beyond logical explanation, a deep attachment (either negatively or positively) which can sometimes be telepathic. Soulmates can be our parents, children, business associates, friends and lovers.

∗

LOVEMATES

Perhaps one of the deepest mysteries within the philosophy of reincarnation is the idea that every human being has a perfect mate waiting to be discovered. This person has been called a lovemate, dualmate, twin flame and sometimes (popularly) a soulmate. Researchers have stated that even in the Stone Age one of the main reasons for leading a useful life was so that one could be reborn near his or her perfect loved one in the next life. The eighteenth-century German writer Johann Wolfgang von Goethe wrote a novel based on the medieval idea that couples were divinely united. The novel, called *Die Wahlverwandt-schaften*, which is usually translated as 'Elective Affinities', contends that every individual has a perfect mate waiting to be discovered.

A commonly held theory regarding lovemates is that we were originally androgynous beings – souls that were neither male nor female. Somewhere in time we were split into two; we became male and female energy (not necessarily male and female bodies). These two halves set forth into the earth plane (a dimension of polarities) to grow and expand, forever striving to reunite. The constant drive towards procreation is seen as a deep spiritual urge for that primal union and for the experience of oneness that occurred before the separation.

Those who hold this theory contend that there will be an increase in the searching for and reuniting with soulmates and lovemates in the coming years because of the increase in the vibratory rate of the planet. This accounts for the rise in non-traditional relationships that transcend differences in race, age, sex, religion and social standing. Some lovemates will be much older or younger than their counterpart, or they will be of different races or socio-economic standing. Yet in the nineties the urge to be together is stronger than society's values. Sometimes one or other of the lovemates can be in the spirit world rather than in a physical body, giving assistance from the 'other side'. This can account for a feeling that some loving presence is watching over you. Lovemates can even be the same sex, though one will usually have the negative (feminine) polarity and the other will have the positive (masculine) polarity.

Lovemates don't always have a relationship that is plain sailing. In fact the relationship can be quite stormy because your lovemate will be your mirror – he or she will emphasize or reflect back to you those areas of yourself with which you aren't satisfied. For that reason, when lovemates come together the relationship isn't always enduring. However, when lovemates truly unite, for whatever length of time, there is a true mating of the heart and the soul that is fathomless.

The degree to which you accept and love yourself is the degree to which you will find your lovemate. If you feel unworthy of love, when you begin to attract your lovemate your mind will say, 'There must be something wrong with this person if he or she loves me.' Then you will subconsciously begin to find things wrong with the other person and push him or her away. Your lovemate can even be your love partner to whom you have been married for twenty years but didn't have the eyes to see.

For many people, the understanding of reincarnation and soulmates answers questions about why we are here. It can give us an understanding of our current relationships, and offer answers to some of life's seemingly unanswerable questions.

*

LAW OF KARMA

Intrinsic to the understanding of reincarnation is the understanding of the oriental concept of karma. 'As ye sow, so shall ye reap' is the principle behind the law of karma. It is the fate we create for ourselves as a result of our judgements of our actions in this life and in previous lives. Karma is the law of cause and effect – the universal law which determines how each of us may weave our own destiny. The idea of karma allows us to understand why one person is dealt adversity all of his life while another seemingly has an easy path. In the past, karma has been viewed as a kind of cosmic accounting system of debits and credits. It was seen as a punitive and retributive law, especially by Westerners. Job in the Bible, suffering the loss of his family and his worldly goods, cried out to God, 'Teach me and I will hold my tongue and cause me to understand wherein I have erred.'

In the past, karma was interpreted as meaning that all suffering was the result of some previous wrongdoing. Anything negative in one's life was thought to be karma-provoked. The blind, the deformed, the lame, the incurable, the suffering were all thought to be paying back for some terrible harm that they had perpetrated in the past. Buddha, however, talked about karma this way: 'The end of it is peace and consummation sweet.' The Hindus talk about karma as a natural and inevitable consequence of every action.

The idea that karma is God's punitive system is changing. There isn't a judge in the clouds who decides what is wrong and what is right for each individual. Instead, I believe that inside of each there is an inner scale of justice monitoring our integrity. It is we who are the judge and jury. It is we who are always trying to balance the scales, instead of a stern deity judging us. Our inner scales deem our actions appropriate or inappropriate, and we are constantly trying to keep these scales in balance. The verdict of these inner scales is not always what we *consciously* assume to be right at the time, even if condoned by religion or society. There are much deeper inner truths to which we adhere – sometimes beyond the rules of society.

I believe that we create not only our reality, but our karma as well. For example, if you cheat someone in a past life and you have not understood or made peace with this memory, then you may feel unworthy and deserving to be punished. Thus, because of your inner need to be punished you create difficult situations around yourself and find yourself being cheated. I don't believe that there is cosmic punishment – only self-punishment. The extent to which you can shift your core beliefs about yourself and the world around you is the extent to which you can step beyond karma.

The Native American View of Karma

In North America the view of karma was slightly different from the Western or even the Eastern view. Conscious acts in life were made by Native Americans with the understanding of how those acts would affect the entire tribe and the following seven generations. If you wanted to cut down a tree, therefore, you would think about how that would affect the seven generations after you. In some tribes, inappropriate acts were not physically punished; instead the offender would take part in numerous discussions with tribal elders until the full consequences of his or her act were understood.

However each tribe dealt with such situations, all Native Americans believed that each and every action affected the whole of life. They intuitively understood that all life and all actions were connected, that we are living in a viable, pulsating, living universe, and that all life is inter-related and interconnecting. The flutter of a butterfly's wings in the Rocky Mountains affects the tornadoes of the Philippines which affects a baby suckling its mother in a small village in Italy. Every act has its consequences. This applies to the physical world as well as to the ways of man: Newton's third law of motion states that every action has its reaction which is equal and opposite.

In the realm of karma, the power of our thoughts is remarkable. Every thought has a life of its own – has form and substance in the causal world. Depending on the intensity, passion and clarity of the mind of the thinker, every thought creates ripples in the fabric of the energy grid of the planet. Actions and words create huge waves of energy that echo throughout the universe. In this way we are constantly creating and balancing karma.

Manifestations of Karma

Karma can manifest itself in different ways. First, it can manifest symbolically. Someone in a past life, who was never willing to see the truth about themselves and the world around them, might be born physically blind in order to be able to perceive truth through intuition and feeling. Someone who, as a Viking warrior, cruelly shed much blood in battle, might develop anaemia. I had a young client who could not swallow very easily. In a past life as a dancer she was forced into a situation that she couldn't swallow.

Karma can also occur as a scale-balancing. For example, a woman who was a lady-in-waiting in the Renaissance always sped through relationships in that past life without taking the time to listen to others. In this life she never feels that anyone is listening to her.

Some afflictions and difficulties don't necessarily come into the 'symbolic' or 'scale-balancing' categories. For example, someone with a physical affliction might incarnate to be of service to other people. A child who is born with Down's Syndrome might be a very evolved being who has incarnated to allow others the 'gift of giving'.

I'm sometimes asked about karma associated with that devastating event, the death of a child. I believe that karmically there are two reasons why a child might die young. The first is that these children have come in service to their family and friends. Whenever a child dies, an enormous amount of soul-searching and a shift of consciousness usually take place for everyone touched by the death. Though incredibly painful, this process usually promotes spiritual growth. I believe that sometimes a child who dies is an evolved soul that doesn't need years on the earth. He or she needs just a short period of physical existence to round off their earth plane experiences. I believe a soul contract is made with the parents and family before the spirit incarnates. Although much pain ensues, powerful spiritual growth arises from going through what must be one of the most difficult experiences on the earth plane.

Instant Karma

Be aware of what you judge in others. Often the very thing that you judge in them will become a part of your life until you accept and forgive the foibles of others. I'll give a very a simple example. One day I was in a grocery store and heard a mother shouting angrily at her young child. I found this very upsetting and thought she was wrong to shout at her child like that. I might have even given her a look that said: 'What you are doing is bad'! Several weeks later I was out shopping and my young daughter was driving me to distraction. I found myself yelling at her. Then suddenly I stopped – in that moment, I was filled with infinite compassion for that other mother. The world is an infinitely better place if we don't judge the actions of others. The Indians would say: 'Walk a mile in my moccasins'.

As the vibratory rate of the planet continues to increase and we each begin to accept more responsibility for our actions, we will find ourselves balancing the scales faster. I call this 'instant karma'. For example, if you judge someone for being inarticulate, the next day you may find yourself in a situation where you feel inarticulate. It is not a punishment, but rather your way of creating a circumstance which will allow you to be more understanding and less judgemental of others. And it will happen faster and faster in the years ahead.

As the planet reaches the end of a long cycle, you will find an increasing momentum towards completion. You will find 'instant karma' occurring more and more often. It's a way of telling how quickly you are growing spiritually. The faster you go, the more instant your thoughts manifest and the faster your judgements will return to you. You will find that the uncompleted relationships and unfinished business of the past (both in this life and in past lives) will move to the forefront for long-awaited completion.

I believe that, because of this speeding up, many people are going through more than one lifetime within this evolutionary cycle. Many people do not want to take the time to become babies, to grow up and to fulfil the karma of just one particular body with the accompanying astrological configurations. They have so much more that they want to complete. Many are going through several lifetimes with one physical body. In the past an individual might be born in a certain village, work at the same occupation as his father and his father before him, marry and die – all in the same village. Now someone might spend half of her life working as a cook in Brazil and the second half in Greece working as a psychologist. Each half of her life could have an entirely different life agenda, and each half could be fulfilling completely different karma.

In any discussion of karma it is important to discuss the view that holds: 'I can't do anything about it. It's my karma.' No matter how difficult the situation in which you are involved in, no matter what difficulties life has dealt you, you are not stuck with your situation. You have free will to change your circumstances or the way that you view them. Your karma hasn't stuck you in unalterable situations. The past, present and future are changeable. You can change your karma and the resulting life circumstances.

*

DESTINY AND FREE WILL

I believe that each of us is born with a predestined future. I believe that the day we are born, our date of death is already decreed. My father's mother was an astrologer who had trained with a remarkable individual named Manly Hall. She said she could see a predilection towards her own death in her astrological chart, and I don't think she was surprised when her time came to leave her body. She believed in predestination.

However, as fervently as I believe in predestination, I also believe in free will. I do not have difficulty in holding two seemingly opposed points of view. In fact I believe that the more opposing points of view you can hold, the more expanded a human being you are. I believe that on any given timeline there is a predestined future *and past*. However, I believe that it is possible to shift in consciousness so that you can choose an entirely different timeline with a new subsequent past and future. In other words, you are not stuck with your past and your future is malleable. (See Chapter 9 for more on future lives.)

In the book *Autobiography of a Yogi*, Paramahansa Yogananda writes about astrology and karma. He states that one's astrological chart can show all the past karma that one has accrued, lifetime after lifetime. He writes: 'A child is born on that day and at that hour when the celestial rays are in mathematical harmony with his individual karma.' He also states that through prayer, spiritual practices and right conduct you can convert difficult karma that might have brought the 'thrust of a sword' to become only the 'thrust of a pin'. However,

Yogananda warns that those astrologers who can accurately decipher your karma from your astrology chart 'are few'.

Not long ago I had some remarkable experiences that make a very solid case for predestination. I was in southern Africa conducting seminars and meeting members of the Zulu tribe. In the course of my travels I met a very special Dutch woman. I was due to go to Holland immediately afterwards and she said that, since she too was going to be in that country at the same time, she would like to cook dinner for me.

When I climbed up the narrow Dutch stairs on the appointed day it was a warm afternoon. The sitting room window was open to the canal below and the small room was filled with sounds from the street. There were metallic sounds of bicycles and the quiet murmurs of conversation from a cafe. Sun reflecting off the canal flooded the room with golden light. Then my new friend began to bring in tray after tray of food. Each bite was filled with magic – the colours, smells and textures all blended together in a rich gastronomic tapestry. When we had finished she said, 'Denise, there is a story I would like to tell you. It is a true story.'

She talked about having spent time in India. During her visits there she heard of a remarkable place in the distant mountains where families descended from a famous astrologer had kept his records for hundreds of years. When the records became too faded they were meticulously copied.

During this astrologer's lifetime, whenever someone consulted him for an astrological reading not only did he do their current chart but he also drew up charts for their future lifetimes! So if you were lucky enough to have been one of his original clients, hundreds of years ago, you could go and find the chart for your present life that had been drawn up hundreds of years before. He told his clients that if they came to retrieve their records in their future life it would be valuable for them.

My first thought was that this sounded almost too unbelievable to be true. I thought perhaps the legend was a ruse to enable money to be taken for the charts, so that members of a poor village could earn a living. When I voiced my thoughts, however, I was told that not only was no one ever charged for the charts, but visitors weren't even allowed to present flowers or gifts.

She decided to travel to the mountains with a friend. When she arrived she told them her birthday and her place of birth. They searched, but told her they were not able to find her chart. They didn't think, therefore, that she was one of the original people who had had their charts prepared hundreds of years before. They did, however, find her friend's chart.

In her friend's present life he had a very painful skin condition. In his chart it said that, during his incarnation in this century, he would have a skin condition that had been acquired because he had not been kind to lepers in his previous life. The chart said that to get rid of the skin condition he must give charitably to leper patients. When he returned home from India he gave some money to charities connected with leprosy, and his skin condition completely cleared up. Eventually he stopped giving to those charities – and his skin problem came back.

I would have regarded this as no more than an interesting story, except that only a month later I heard a similar tale. I was in London giving a series of lectures on reincarnation when I was asked to take part in a BBC radio programme in which guests from different backgrounds participated in a lively discussion of varied topics. One of the other guests was a man who originally came from India. At the end of the show this very soft-spoken Indian gentleman, a doctor and sculptor, said, 'There is something that I would like to show you.'

As we sat in the lobby he pulled out a sheaf of faded papers torn at the edges. The pages were covered in what I assumed to be the ancient Eastern language Sanskrit. The doctor then proceeded to tell a most unusual story. When he was nineteen he had travelled with his father to a place where astrological records had been kept for hundreds of years. It sounded like the same place that had been described to me in Amsterdam. After a very long and arduous journey, they arrived on a rainy day – a very unusual occurrence in that part of the world. They went to see if they could locate the astrological charts for their present lives, and both he and his father found that they had indeed been clients of the famous astrologer hundreds of years before. The doctor told me that his chart said that he would come to claim his records when he was nineteen, and on a rainy day. His chart also quoted correctly his name in his present life. As we looked over his well-worn chart I said, 'You've had this chart for some thirty years. Has it been accurate?' He went carefully through the chart with me (though I only had his word for what it said, as I cannot read Sanskrit) and showed me many examples of where it had been very accurate.

I pass these stories along to you as they were shared with me. I found both individuals to be very honest, trustworthy people. I believe them, and I believe the stories that they told me.

*

TRANSMIGRATION

I'm often asked if we have always been human beings in past lives. I have found that it is not unusual for individuals spontaneously to 'remember' a lifetime as an animal, for example, if they have come from cultures where the predominant religious belief is based on reincarnation. This is especially true when part of the cultural belief entails the transmigration of souls into animal bodies. People whom I have regressed who are originally from native cultures also seem to have a predilection towards recalling a past life as an animal. I find it very unusual for someone from our Western culture to recall a life as an animal in a past life regression. I don't think this means that Westerners haven't had animal lives whereas people from native cultures have. I believe that, since they live closer to the earth, native peoples are more in tune with the reality of nature and so they are more likely to *remember* past lives as an animal. Westerners are so out of touch with the cycles of nature that they are less likely to do so. I believe that there isn't anything out there that isn't you anyway, so I don't preclude past lives as animals.

Let me tell you a true story that gives credence to humans

having had past lives as animals. My years in the Zen Buddhist monastery were a very austere time. We were required to sit in meditation in the lotus or half lotus position for up to sixteen hours a day. During meditation we sat facing a bare wall within the monastery. We weren't allowed to have our eyes open, for the Zen masters felt that might be distracting and we might be tempted to look around. But we weren't allowed to close our eyes either, for they felt that we might be tempted to go to sleep or we might start visualizing instead of doing our meditation practice. We were required to have our eyes half-open in an unfocused gaze at the wall. When we sat, our backs had to be ramrod straight and we weren't allowed to move.

In these circumstances it was easy to be distracted by pain or tiredness. So as an act of compassion, with lightning accuracy, the Zen master would strike the shoulder of a Zen practitioner with a kyôsaku stick to ensure attentiveness in his discipline. A kyôsaku stick is similar to a flat baseball bat or a cricket stump. The Catch-22 of this practice was that if the Zen master deemed that you were doing really well, he would smack just as hard in order to encourage you!

In the quiet of the monastery inner demons from our subconscious or from our past would rise into our awareness. This was uncomfortable and often took great courage to face. We were told by the Zen masters that, no matter what we saw or experienced during our meditation, it was all 'maya' (an illusion). We were told to detach ourselves from it. I don't know if this is the best psychological way to deal with emotional difficulties, but as this was the way it was done in the Zen Buddhist tradition for hundreds of years we accepted it.

One of the most avid of my fellow Zen students was called Chuck. One day, perhaps overwhelmed by the difficulty of the monastic practices, he committed suicide. While living at the monastery I had adopted a stray white cat, which shortly after Chuck's death had six pure white kittens. One of the kittens had one blue eye and one green eye. *Chuck had one blue eye and one green eye.* One day the kitten with one blue eye and one green eye fell off the top of the garage, injured a leg and began to walk with a limp. *Chuck had walked with a limp.* When all the kittens were old enough to be out chasing butterflies and scampering through the monastery gardens we noticed something very unusual. Every time the gong was sounded to begin meditation, the kitten with the two different-coloured eyes would run to the door nearest the meditation room. (Cats were not allowed inside the monastery.) This very solemn kitten would sit absolutely still outside the door for the entire lengthy meditation. This occurred day after day and seemed very unusual for a young kitten which one would have expected to be active and playful. We couldn't help but wonder if that kitten had been our friend Chuck. The kitten, in fact, did seem very attentive whenever we talked to her, and she particularly responded to the name that we gave her – Chuckee.

Chuck was a very enlightened man, so perhaps after he died he felt that he didn't want to take the time to incarnate into a human body and have to go through all the effort of growing up. Perhaps he came back in a cat's body to gain just a little physicalness before going on to the next stage of his development. Perhaps it will be a long time before I will know the whole story, but I do think it is possible that we have lives other than human.

Understanding the philosophy of reincarnation is helpful in understanding your personal past lives. When you can view your past lives in the larger context of reincarnation and karma, the many pieces of the puzzle as to why you are here on earth at this time in history, and what your purpose is, will begin to fall into place.

3

*

Past Life Therapy

You do not have to believe in reincarnation for past life therapy to be beneficial in your life; it can work whether or not you believe. Many of my clients didn't believe in reincarnation, yet they gained immense value from the therapy. Although I have had clients who researched the uncovered past life information and found that the lives they 'saw' were historically factual, to try to prove that the images that are in a person's mind are actual memories isn't as important as the results. When someone's life changes by experiencing images in their mind, true healing has occurred. Even if the images that come to the surface are simply symbols of the subconscious mind, they deserve to be heard. They are legitimate expressions of our inner being and can expand the quality of our lives.

Past life therapy can sometimes give answers that neither traditional medicine nor traditional therapy provide. Of course, there can be many contributing reasons for our problems in life. It can be all too easy to blame present problems on past life behaviour. Nevertheless, past life exploration has proved incredibly powerful in many cases where regular introspection into present life circumstances has failed to bring changes. Understanding our place and mission in the present can be helped through understanding what we have been in previous lives. Life is not a one-time affair; it is not a series of meaningless experiences strung together. Past life exploration can assist the process of emerging as a conscious, loving being, gradually realizing our full potential.

*

HEALTH

Delving into past lives during therapy can positively affect all aspects of life. An area that I have found responds particularly well for me is health problems.

Karen was a client who came to me because she thought she was sabotaging herself from being in a long-term, loving relationship; she also felt she had a weight problem. Although there is not necessarily a connection between weight and relationships, Karen felt there was for her. She was a thirty-ish well-dressed woman who was 30 pounds overweight, and felt that her size was a contributory factor in preventing her from enjoying a long-term, satisfying relationship.

In her past life therapy she vividly remembered a life as a prostitute in eighteenth-century England. She recalled the bitter cold of the London streets, the occasional frantic encounter with a customer and long, hungry days. She was very unhappy in that life. In her regression she relived the grief at being stuck in a profession that she considered harmful to her. More important, during the regression she got in touch with a belief that she had formed at the time. Karen's belief was, 'If I'm attractive, men will desire me for my body and I will feel cheap and degraded.' She came forward into this life with that belief embedded in her 'bio-energy matrix'. Each of us has what I call a bio-energy matrix. This is your personal energy field that is made up of all the different aspects of your energy fields. These aspects include your emotional body, your astral body, your etheric body and your bio-electrical system (this is the meridian system that acupuncture works on). Beliefs, decisions and judgements are not just lodged in your brain. I believe that they are in fact also lodged in your physical body and in the myriad of energy fields that superimpose your body. I call these energy fields together your 'bio-energy matrix'.

In her regression, Karen discovered that even though consciously she wanted to feel attractive and she desired a relationship, subconsciously she was afraid that if she felt attractive men would be attracted to her and she would be degraded again. This core belief had been controlling her life since she was a child. Any time a man was attracted to her, she would subconsciously feel afraid and sabotage any hope of a relationship.

During the regression she was able to release her old belief, and her entire life changed as a result. She embraced a new belief about herself that stated: 'I can feel and be attractive. People are attracted to me for who I am. Who I am is special.' Almost immediately she started to lose those 30 pounds of excess weight, but more importantly she began to feel good about herself. Karen is now happily married, and looking and feeling attractive. (See Chapter 6 for past life resolution techniques.)

A young man named John came to me for a regression. He had had a physical problem for many years: he couldn't perspire – his sweat glands didn't seem to work. His skin was dry and he was very uncomfortable. He had tried numerous medical drugs, to no avail. He regressed to a time when he had been a servant at a Russian court. As a servant John was required to stand at attention for hours during lengthy banquets in case guests wanted anything. During one important banquet he had a very full bladder, but he knew he wasn't allowed to leave his post. Eventually he lost control of his bladder and at the same time ran out of the banqueting hall. In a subsequent fit of anger his master killed him.

In the regression John discovered a subconscious belief that he should hold back body excretions or he wouldn't survive. His body translated this idea in such a way that he stopped perspiring. As soon as he discovered the source of his difficulty and resolved it, immediately (during the session) his sweat glands began to work. And they have done so ever since.

*

RELATIONSHIPS

Past life regression can also help us understand relationships. A daughter who resents her mother telling her what to do may find that in a past life their roles were reversed: the present daughter was the mother, and her mother the child. The present daughter may never have got over the feeling that *she* should be in charge, not the other way around. Remembering and understanding why she feels the way she does about her mother can help her to create a more accepting relationship where she is not being run by her past programming.

Sue had worked at the same job for seven years. Almost every day during those seven years she was angry with her boss. He noticed every detail of her job and she almost felt he was suffocating her. In her regression she discovered a past life where her boss had been her husband – who was not attentive at all. They had been pioneers in Montana in the 1800s and had lived in a small mountain cabin miles from any other habitation. In that life as a pioneer wife, Sue was very lonely and wanted company. Her husband used to leave their cabin, sometimes for weeks at a time, to go hunting and exploring. She used to complain that he wasn't very attentive. On one occasion when he was away, Sue was caught in a landslide behind the cabin and suffocated to death.

When Sue realized that her boss, in their present life, was trying to make up for being inattentive in their past life she forgave him (while she was regressed) for not being attentive to her. She also let him know it wasn't his fault that she had suffocated. Even though she never told her boss about her regression, she said that from that day forward he seemed completely changed. Even the other office workers noticed the difference. He seemed much more relaxed and at ease with her, and everyone in the office enjoyed the benefits of his more relaxed mood.

*

ABUNDANCE

Whenever Mark began to start to get ahead financially, he would back down from success. He was never quite able to make ends meet for his family. A common expression of Mark's was, 'We are poor but we are happy.' When he regressed to a past life he saw that he had been a wealthy landowner in the Middle Ages. His family had been taken and held for ransom by a group of marauding bandits. His young wife (who happened to be his wife in this life) was never seen again by him in that life.

He recalled night after night, slouched in damp quarters in his manor house, blaming himself and his wealth for the loss of his wife. This subconscious guilt carried forward into his present life: he felt that if he had too much money his family would be taken from him. This belief was so strong that if he ever did make money he would most likely become separated from his family physically and emotionally to support his subconscious belief. After Mark recognized this belief pattern, a remarkable financial change occurred. He was quickly given a promotion, as he was no longer sabotaging his advancement, and interestingly enough he went into the property market. As a result he made a very nice annual gain and he and his family now live very well.

*

ACTIVATING TALENTS AND ABILITIES

An exciting area of past life regression is the activation of past life talents and abilities for use in the present life. Rob came to one of my seminars and regressed to a time when he had played the violin. The following week he bought a violin and enrolled for a course of lessons. He reported that his teacher was astounded at how quickly and easily he was able to learn.

Carolyn had always wanted to sing but felt that she didn't have a very good voice – she said people used to tease her about it. After she experienced a past life in which she had been an excellent singer she said that it seemed almost magical how quickly her voice had improved. Now she sings in a choir in her home town.

In my seminars I often do a past life process specifically aimed at activating talents, abilities and qualities from past lives. At the end of one of these processes a women came up to me and said, 'I don't understand. In my past life experience I saw that I was a shepherd. All I did every day was spend time in the hills by myself, occasionally herding sheep. What talent or ability is that?'

I said, 'Tell me about your present life.'

She answered, 'Well, I'm pretty busy in my life because I have six kids.' She had activated a life where she had experienced tremendous peace. I believe she tuned into that particular life so she could bring some of that peace into her present hectic life.

I've developed a technique in my seminars that seems to help bring a particular talent or ability into present life. While the participants are in a state of altered consciousness with their eyes closed, experiencing a talented past life, I ask them to move or position their body as if they were participating in their particular talent. For example, when Rob recalled a life as a violinist while his eyes were closed, I asked him to stand up and move his arms and body just as if he were playing a violin. In this way be began to understand what it feels like to play the violin. This kind of thing helps the body remember how to do the particular activity. Moving the body while experiencing a past life actually helps to 'implant' that special quality into your present-life physical body.

In one of my seminars when I was leading this particular past life talent process I saw a young man in the corner of the hall doing what looked like push-ups. I assumed that he must have been a very good athlete in another life, and that he was doing push-ups to bring his past athletic abilities into present time. During the break I asked him what past life talent he had encountered. His face turned red as he lowered his voice and whispered, 'I was a great lover!' I can only hope that his love-making abilities have improved as a result of his sojourn into the past.

*

RELEASING THE FEAR OF DEATH

Another benefit of past life regression is the release of the fear of death, enabling you to live much more fully and intensely. When you really experience the fact that you are infinite and eternal, and that *you* don't die when your body dies, you begin to experience a deep inner peace that pervades everyday activities. The thought of dying can be frightening or extremely sad to someone who thinks that this one life is all there is.

Mitchell had AIDS. He had never had very strong religious beliefs, and was terrified of dying. He thought that existence just stopped at that point. He didn't believe in reincarnation, but a friend persuaded him to come and see me. Because of his uncertainty about past lives I told him that he didn't have to believe in reincarnation. I said we could do a past life process and call the images he saw 'soul dramas' instead of past lives. I told him that the images he would experience were a valid expression of his subconscious mind, and that whether they were past lives or symbolic expressions of his inner psyche wasn't important – those inner messages deserved to be heard no matter where they came from. He could accept that point of view. ('Soul dramas', incidentally, is a term originated by my friend Roger Woolger, an excellent past life therapist and writer on the subject.)

Very quickly Mitchell went into a deep relaxed state. The images and feelings of other times and other places came very easily to him. Suddenly he had a spontaneous experience seemingly unsolicited by anything I said. He said that he 'saw' all the bodies that he had ever inhabited in all his lifetimes coming forward like a great gathering of friends. Some were male, some were female. Many different races were represented. As he stood in the centre of this gathering, one by one these past 'selves' came forward and told him what he gained from each life. Finally the body that looked exactly like his present one came forward and said, 'Each life allows you a greater and deeper understanding of who you are in your entirety. Each life is special, important and valuable. The body and the life that you are currently inhabiting is allowing you to develop your ability to receive love. You are learning this lesson well, and soon you will be going home.' At this point Mitchell began to sob. It seemed that a dam of uncertainty and fear and pain was released as he cried. When he stopped sobbing, he smiled and said, 'I have never felt such a seep sense of peace. I am ready to go when it is my time.' He died a few weeks later, but I was told that his last few weeks of life were filled with a profound grace and peace.

*

WHY PAST LIFE THERAPY WORKS

It is important to understand why using past life regression in conjunction with therapy is so healing. Past life therapy works because it allows you to get to the source of your problem; until then you are dealing with symptoms rather than causes. Many of our fears, compulsions and phobias are rooted in the distant past. For example, if you have always hated wearing anything tight around your neck, you may discover a lifetime in which you were choked to death. By recognizing and experiencing the past memories and the associated emotions, the present life behaviour frequently changes.

We create and recreate for ourselves present-day incidents that subconsciously remind us of the original incident as a way to heal the original pain. If emotions such as fear, anger or grief are suppressed during traumatic events in a past life, these suppressed emotions stay inside our energy field and form inner conflicts that continue lifetime after lifetime. We continue to push these undesired feelings from the past deeper into our psyche, building a greater and greater barrier between ourselves and whatever we are afraid to feel. When you re-experience a past life incident, the emotions and decisions that were suppressed for so long have the opportunity to come to the surface and release themselves, so that they are no longer controlling you.

To understand why past life therapy works it's important to understand that it is not necessarily the trauma and the emotions that you experienced in your past lives that create problems in your present life. It is the trauma and emotions that were *suppressed* in the past that create difficulties in the present. Your past life experiences do not necessarily create continuing problems – it is your *reactions* to those experiences and your blocked emotions that create the havoc. For example, just falling down a ravine in a past life won't necessarily create a blockage in present life, but falling down a ravine while feeling emotional anguish can.

Joshua experienced a past life in which he had been a young man in medieval Europe. He remembered telling his trusted friends at the time that, contrary to the accepted belief, he thought that the King wasn't directly descended from God. His friends were furious and chased him, causing him to fall down a ravine. As he fell, he was in a turmoil. He loved his friends, yet his feelings of love were at odds with his fear of them while they chased him. As he fell, he made a decision that he would never again share his feelings honestly.

In Joshua's present life he had always been afraid to speak his mind. In fact, often when he began to say what he really felt he physically tripped and fell. Joshua had an inner subconscious association between speaking his mind and falling. It wasn't the physical trauma of falling in a past life that caused him to have present-day blockages. The suppressed emotions and feelings and decisions made at the time that he fell in the Middle Ages created his current problems. Joshua was able to change his lifelong pattern by using the past life resolution techniques in Chapter 6, and says that he now feels very confident in his life. He can now communicate what he really feels without fear.

Imagine two similar scenarios. In the first scenario a young Aztec warrior is fighting alongside his best friend. The dust is churning. Spears are flying on either side of the gallant warrior. Suddenly in the haze of battle a spear comes straight for the chest of the friend. The young warrior magnificently steps in front of the spear, valiantly saving the life of his friend. As he dies, mortally wounded by a spear thrust to the chest, he feels a deep peace for he has saved his friend's life.

In the second scenario two young warriors are battling side by side. They are best friends. Suddenly in the thrall of battle, obscured by the thick haze and dust, one turns to the other and thrusts a spear into his chest. As the warrior lies dying on the battlefield he learns that his best friend is having an affair with his wife and wants him out of the way. He dies making a decision that you can never really trust anyone.

In both scenarios the physical trauma is the same. Death is caused by a spear wound to the chest. However in the first instance the Aztec warrior feels exhilaration at having saved the life of his friend. In the second scenario, however, he decides it's not safe to trust anyone. Henceforth, whenever he begins to get close to someone early similar memories and decisions are activated. Whenever he begins to trust someone he experiences severe chest pains in conjunction with a fear of being betrayed. For him, getting close to someone activated an emotional and physical response from a past life.

*

THE ROLE OF THE SUBCONSCIOUS AND PAST LIFE THERAPY

'You are what you think.' This doesn't refer simply to what you *know* you think. It also refers to what you *don't know* you think. For example, you may be unaware that deep inside your subconscious lie fears and beliefs that you are perhaps unworthy and don't deserve success in life. These fears and beliefs set up inner blocks to fulfilment and create frustration in life. There's a good reason why this is so. It has to do with the fact that your subconscious mind exerts a far greater control over your life than you can possibly realize. It literally directs your reality. Imagine a plane that is flying straight towards a mountainside in the fog. The control tower (the conscious mind) can be yelling: 'Turn back! Turn back!' But unless the subconscious mind (the pilot) gets the message, the plane will crash into the mountain.

Often people wonder why the subconscious ever accepts self-defeating programming in the first place. After all, don't we want the very best for ourselves? Don't we all really want to be healthy, happy and successful? The answers to these questions lie in the nature of the subconscious mind. Although your conscious mind has the ability to reason and decide what would be best for you, it cannot implement any decision unless the subconscious mind agrees. An alcoholic may consciously want to give up drinking, yet he will continue to drink despite his conscious mind's desperate desire to stop. Our subconscious acts the way that it has been programmed to act in much the same way that a computer is programmed.

For example, a small child's mother might say, 'You're so clumsy. You have no rhythm. You'll never be able to dance.' The child's critical faculties are not developed enough to reject this negative programming, so she may grow up being very clumsy with no sense of rhythm because the subconscious has accepted the idea of clumsiness. In other words, clumsiness has been programmed into the computer-like subconscious. This idea then becomes an integral part of the child's view of herself. As an adult she might reason that she doesn't need to be clumsy and with enough training will be able to dance. However, if the conscious mind proposes a belief that is different from the subconscious programming, the subconscious mind will be the dominant mind.

The subconscious mind also functions on behalf of our survival. For example, if you were bitten by a barking dog when you were four years old, your subconscious mind would probably programme a fear of barking dogs into its computer. As an adult, if you came upon a barking dog (even if it were a very small dog tied with a heavy chain) you would most likely feel momentary fear because a fear of barking dogs had been pre-programmed into your subconscious mind to protect you – to ensure your survival. Your conscious mind may know that you are safe, but the programming is so strongly embedded into the subconscious that you react with fear.

Not only does your subconscious mind accept programming from early childhood, but it also accepts programming from past lives. For example, I had a client who was terrified of bees and would become almost paralysed when she saw just one. She had been stung to death by bees in a past life, so her subconscious mind, wanting to ensure her survival, made a decision to stay away from bees. Even though the conscious mind says, 'It's just a little bee. You are much bigger and stronger,' the subconscious mind takes precedence.

The subconscious mind is so powerful that beliefs from early childhood and past lives become 'glued' into your energy field. These subconscious beliefs coalesce into form in the manifest world. This means that your entire world is created or manifested by the *core* beliefs in your subconscious about yourself and life. For example, if you have a core belief that all your romantic relationships will fail, you will continue to create relationships that fail – even though you consciously want to be in a long-lasting, loving relationship. Past life therapy works by using specific techniques to reach deep into the subconscious mind and literally reprogram old beliefs and decisions that are influencing every aspect of life. (See Chapter 6 for past life resolution techniques.)

∗

NO VICTIMS – JUST VOLUNTEERS

It's important to remember that when you connect with your past life (either through your dreams or in waking consciousness) there are no victims – just volunteers. Every experience that you have had was necessary for your growth and for you to get where you are now. As uncomfortable as it may sound, every lie you ever told and every nasty thing that you did or that was done to you was necessary for your own learning. Remember this if you come up with a lifetime in which you were either a victim or a tyrant.

I imagine the victim/volunteer scenario going something like this. You are walking around in the spirit world. You've examined your past lives and decide, for your next incarnation, that it would be valuable, for your evolution as a human being, to learn some humility. You begin to grab passing spirits. 'Hey, I'm about to incarnate. Why don't you incarnate too and teach me some humility?' The spirits all shy away from you, saying, 'No way! I'm not going to mess up my karmic evolution teaching you humility.'

Then finally shuffling up to the Pearly Gates comes Harry, an old acquaintance. Harry is someone whom you have shared lifetime after lifetime with – someone whom you love deeply on a soul level. 'Hey, Harry, I really need to learn humility. How about it?' And Harry shrugs, lovingly puts his arm around you and agrees.

Those individuals who have victimized you the most are the very ones who love you the most deeply on a soul level. In my regression work I have discovered, time and time again, that after processing the grief and rage and bitterness that we hold towards our victimizers there is, almost always an enormous well of love.

＊

FORGIVING PAST LIFE CIRCUMSTANCES

One of the most powerful things that you can gain from past life therapy is forgiveness. Often, to be able to heal, you must be willing to forgive the past. It is much easier to forgive those who have wounded you in your present life when you understand the past life karma that precipitated the situation. When you travel to the source of your woundedness, which often lies in a past life, and forgive yourself and forgive others, a loving energy weaves its way through time and space to your present life. It goes without saying that it is important to forgive those who may have hurt or denied you in a past life; however, it is just as important to forgive yourself for those things which you may have done to others. (If you have difficulty letting go and forgiving, you must forgive yourself for not forgiving.)

Often, when someone has regressed to a past life, they reach a space beyond forgiveness – a space where they realize that everything that ever happened in life was absolutely necessary for growth and development. In fact, without those experiences they would not be who they are today. The plane beyond forgiveness is acceptance – total unconditional acceptance without judging yourself or anyone else. I find this one of the most healing aspects of past life therapy.

I am often asked if my past life explorations have allowed me to discover why I was so brutally attacked. Yes, I have found some satisfactory answers. Using past life exploration to understand my karmic connection with the man who shot me helped me to forgive him. I shared a life in China with him. All the people in our small village lived in houses that were built up off the ground. The villagers placed body wastes through holes in the floor into containers underneath the houses. Every morning, a man (the man who shot me) would come and clear away the waste from beneath the houses. This character was more or less an 'untouchable', with no social standing in the community. Though my extreme disdain for him in that life was a minor thing to me, it was major to him. Just as in this life, shooting me was for him only a matter of slight concern (it is believed that he had killed a number of people), it was a major concern for me. We had a slight, yet intense karmic connection. I had never seen him before I was shot, and I only saw him once (at the trial) after I was shot.

When I realized my past life connection with this man, I finally understood why my last thought before I was hit was: 'He's aiming too low!' I had a subconscious desire to balance the karma of having treated him so cruelly in that past life. (If he had aimed any higher, he would have killed me.) Through discovering my past connection with this individual, I was able to forgive him and accept what had happened, thus harbouring no resentment that could be carried into my present relationships.

Some of the most rewarding comments I get after past life seminars relate to forgiving present life and past life circumstances. In Australia I conducted a past life process in a seminar in the Japanese-owned Nikko Hotel. I received an interesting letter from someone who attended that seminar, who said that on entering the hotel an intense wave of resentment and panic came over her. She thought, 'I can't attend this seminar in *this* hotel', and almost turned and fled.

In her current life she had been taken prisoner in Indonesia by the Japanese in World War II when she was seventeen. She said in her letter that she had 'suffered physically as well as mentally from their brutality during the rest of the war. I survived, but my intestines were damaged from untreated dysentery. I was severely undernourished and I harboured a deep hatred for everything Japanese. This has continued ever since. I have sought treatment from many physicians and psychologists during the last fifty years, but I have had to live with a chronic weakness of the bowel and a deep constant pain in the solar plexus.' She said she had come to see the pain as the pain in the centre of her being which she carried for all reviled beings in the world. She continued, 'Whenever I see or read about instances of brutality and inhumanity against others – especially children – the pain becomes almost unbearable.'

My correspondent said that after she regressed into a past life in the seminar she was able to see the source of current life resentment (she didn't mention what the past life was) and, as a result of forgiving past life circumstances, the pain which had plagued her for fifty years had completely lifted. 'This old pain has disappeared and today I'm still free of it. When I left the hotel I gave a friendly greeting to the Japanese staff.' She said she spent time talking to some of them and found them to be very pleasant, lovely people, 'I feel free! Free from pain! Free from all animosity and all resentment! Truly and gloriously free and easy!'

Another seminar participant, Gerald, had a vicious relationship with his brother in his current life. As they were growing up his mother was concerned that the two brothers might kill each other because they fought so ferociously. The animosity had continued into adult life and was causing great upheaval for the entire family. In addition, Gerald felt that his hatred was taking up so much of his life energy that it was holding him back from being a success in life.

Gerald regressed to a life in sixteenth-century Scandinavia, where he and his present-day brother had been rivals for the same woman. He 'remembered' that one cold, snowy afternoon they had fought over this woman, but neither had won her hand because they had both died from their injuries. In his present life he was recreating a similar scenario. When he truly forgave his rival in his past life regression, he said he felt as though a huge weight had lifted from his shoulders. It seemed like a miracle to him, he told me, because the next time he saw his brother he felt only love and compassion for him. For the first time in their lives they sat down together and truly shared from their hearts. Gerald said it was a turning point in his life, and he is now beginning to succeed in his career as well as healing lifelong wounds.

*

'WE DON'T KNOW THE WHOLE STORY'

To help you understand and forgive what you have done to others in past lives and what others have done to you, there is a story that I would like to share with you. I tell it often in my seminars. Some say it is an old Sufi story, while others say it came from India. Here's my version.

A long time ago an old man lived in a village. He had an extremely beautiful horse. All the people in the villages across the land had heard of this horse. It was a magnificent animal with long, shining loins. Its muscles rippled with sheen and glory every time it moved.

The Great Chief heard of this horse and sent a messenger to

the old man asking if he could purchase it. The warrior messenger raced to the old man's teepee and jumped down from his horse. Where his moccasins landed, the dust swirled in all directions. 'Old man, I am here on behalf of the Great Chief. He sends his greetings and asks that he may buy your horse.'

The old man was silent. He was a man of gentle dignity and quiet manners. Finally he said, 'Please give my regards to the Great Chief, and please thank him for his kind offer to buy my horse. However, this horse is my friend. We are companions. I know his soul as I feel he knows mine. I cannot sell my friend.' The messenger rode away.

Two weeks later the old man's horse disappeared.

When the villagers heard that the horse was missing they all gathered around the old man. 'Oh, old man, this is very bad fortune! You could have sold your horse to the Great Chief. Now you have no horse and no payment for the horse. What bad fortune!'

The old man looked at each villager with kind, soft eyes and said, 'It is not bad fortune. It is not good fortune. We don't know the whole story. Just say the horse ran away.' The villagers went away shaking their heads because they knew that this was very bad fortune.

A month later the old man's horse returned, followed by twenty other magnificent horses. Each one was spirited and bursting with vitality and exuberance. The villagers ran forward to the old man. 'Oh, old man. You were right – it was not bad fortune that your horse ran away. It was good fortune. Now not only do you have your horse back but you have twenty more beautiful horses. This is good fortune!'

The old man slowly shook his head and with utmost compassion said, 'It is not good. It is not bad. We don't know the whole story. Just say that the horse returned.' The people went away shaking their heads. They knew that it was very, very good fortune to have so many beautiful horses.

The old man had one son who started to break in the horses. Every day the son would wake early to continue his work. One morning the old man came to watch his son. The young man had a natural grace as he swung on to the bare back of a wild

Pinto. The horse bucked violently to the left and twisted to the right. Suddenly with a ferocious kick of his hind legs the Pinto tossed the son high in the air. The old man's son landed in a crumpled heap in the dust. Both of his legs were broken.

All the inhabitants of the village gathered with great moaning and commiserating. 'Oh, no! Oh, no! Old man, you are right. Your horse returning to you was very bad fortune. Now your only son has both legs broken and is crippled. Who is going to take care of you in your old age? This is very bad fortune.'

The old man pulled himself upright and with respect said, 'It is not bad fortune. It is not good fortune. Just say my son broke his legs. We don't know the whole story.' The villagers walked away, shaking their heads. They knew it was very bad fortune for the old man.

A great war broke out across the land and the Great Chief called all the young men of the villages to battle. It was a bad war and the villagers knew they would never see their sons again. Once more they gathered around the old man. 'Old man, you are right. It is not bad fortune that your son broke his legs because, even though he is crippled, you have your son. We will never see our sons again. It was good fortune for you.'

And once again the old man said, 'It is not good fortune. It is not bad fortune. We don't know the whole story.'

As you explore your past lives there will be times when you will experience yourself as the victim and times when you experience yourself as the victimizer. Step beyond right and wrong. Step beyond judgement. Know that who and what you have been and what you have experienced in the past is not good . . . It is not bad. You might not always know the whole story.

Every experience that you have ever had, *everything* that has been done to you and *everything* that you have done to others has been extremely important for your evolution. Even those lies that you told or those times when you were cruel or unjust have been important. Even those things that reside in shame in your soul have helped you to become who you are. All your experiences are helping you to be compassionate, whole and loving. To the extent that you can forgive and accept yourself exactly as you are you become a more powerful force for healing on the planet. Remember: 'It is not good. It is not bad. You might not know the whole story.' Every experience that you have ever had has allowed you to grow towards becoming a magnificent being.

*

RELEASING GUILT

In the mid-seventies I took a trip to Italy. One morning I got up early to walk to a hill to watch the sun rise. As the first spears of light thrust over the horizon I was overwhelmed with a deep sadness. In my mind's eye, as I looked over the valley, I was seeing not a twentieth-century scene but another time. I 'saw' smoke residue from numerous small camp fires rising and mixing with the morning mists. I could 'see' that no one was up as yet. As I stood on that hill, I 'knew' that I had been there before. I 'knew' I was the Roman commander of a large army – an army that had been fighting for a long time.

Asleep by their camp fire, there were not just men in the valley below me, but also women and even some children. I felt wave after wave of grief fill me. I knew that this would be our last battle. Rather than surrender, I made the decision that we would fight our last battle on that day. I knew that I would have to speak to the troops with conviction of our victory. But I also knew that it was the day of our deaths. I knew that we would be killed without mercy. But the alternative was imprisonment, starvation or slavery for my people. 'What might I have done differently?' These were my people. I loved my people. Perhaps if I had been a better leader we wouldn't be facing death. These questions were superimposed on my present-day consciousness that early morning.

Twenty years later, the incident in Italy was only a wisp of a memory. I was leading a reincarnation seminar in New Zealand. One of the organizers had brought her young son along to help her, and he decided to participate in one of the past life processes. During the break he came up to me and said with soft sadness, 'Denise, do you remember when we were Romans? Do you remember when we were on a hillside looking at the smoke rise from the camp fires from the night before?'

A year later someone who had never heard of my experience on that hillside said, 'Denise, do you remember when we were together in Italy as Roman soldiers? You were the commander. I fought alongside you at the last battle. It was magnificent. We all fought so gallantly, It was one of the most powerful experiences of all my lifetimes.'

I was astounded! He not only remembered the same life, but stated that he felt exhilarated by the experience. It was a powerful lesson for me: 'I don't always know the whole story.' I had felt so guilty about contributing to the deaths of so many people. I had punished myself lifetime after lifetime. I felt responsible for the experiences of others and had even presupposed what those experiences were. I could see that I no longer needed to carry guilt around – and in fact feeling guilty was arrogant.

Each individual creates the experience that is valuable for them and their growth. I didn't need to continue to shoulder guilt for everyone else. We *all* jointly created the experience of the last battle. This might sound like a subtle realization, but for me, in my life, it made a huge difference. Until then I had felt guilty for just about everything. I even felt guilty for things over which I had no control. If you came and told me that you had dented your car by backing into a post, most likely *I* would feel guilty. To begin to release guilt was so freeing.

A common occurrence when one has a disturbing dream or has encountered a disturbing past life is to feel guilty about your experiences. It is important to remember that there is never any cause for guilt in any dream or past life experience that you encounter. Release any censorship of yourself.

Guilt is basically not taking responsibility for your actions. Guilt is a way of saying: 'I really didn't do it. It really isn't my fault.' It is important to acknowledge all your actions, without judgement. If you have hurt someone, make it right. If you have behaved inappropriately, alter your behaviour. But do not dishonour the situation, the other person or yourself by feeling guilty.

Guilt is always disruptive, and sometimes arrogant. Forgive yourself your past. When you maintain that you are guilty and your source of guilt lies in the past, you are not looking inward. To look inward is to know that everything that you have ever experienced was necessary for your growth and understanding. It was necessary in order for you to be who you are today. Even the thoughts and actions you may be ashamed of contributed to your being who you are today. As uncomfortable as those memories are, it is important to observe and release them. Forgive yourself. Any residue of guilt that you still cling to can be creating barriers for you. It can often be processed and released in your dreams (see page 117).

Whenever the pain of guilt seems to attract you, remember this. If you yield to it instead of forgiving yourself, you are deciding against inner peace. Therefore, say to yourself gently, but with conviction, 'I accept who I am and what I have done as well as what others have done to me. I accept and forgive myself.'

One valuable technique is to write down all your feelings of guilt. After you have written them all down, burn them, saying, 'I release now and for evermore my attachments to this guilt. So be it.' This may begin to help release guilt.

Past life therapy can be one of the fastest ways to release guilt, to forgive the past and to heal present-day problems. Chapter 4 shows you various methods of recalling your past lives.

4

*

How to
Recall
a Past Life

*T*here are numerous techniques that you can use by yourself
or with a therapist to explore past lives. In this chapter
you will be shown specific techniques to use on your own,
including preparatory exercises as well as full regression process techniques. I also discuss working with a therapist or in a
group to recall your past lives. I shall start by describing some
of the methods you can use initially to explore the direction in
which your past lives have gone, without going into a full
regression. Then I shall share several in-depth processes for
completing a full regression and learning exactly what experiences may be lingering from the past and affecting your present
life. Whenever you do any of the exercises I describe, I strongly
recommend that you carefully monitor the feelings which come
up for you, and that you seek the support of a friend or trained
therapist whenever you feel you need to. I shall discuss what to
look for in a therapist later in this chapter.

It can be very helpful to talk out whatever comes up for you,
whether it is painful or joyous. Sharing the work you are doing
with someone who is close to you in this life is a wonderful and
important way to integrate material from past lives into your
present experience. Just be sure to choose this companion carefully – make sure it is someone who truly cherishes you and will
not make light of the important work you are setting out to do.

*

JUST MAKING IT UP

People in my past life therapy seminars will sometimes say, 'But I'm just making this up!' when they get in touch with a past life during a process. Of course you are making it up. Where do you think all of life came from? You are always 'making it up', no matter what you are experiencing. Just let go. Allow your imagination free rein without constantly questioning the images, and you will begin to receive more and more accurate information regarding your past. When you first begin to try to discover your past lives the images are often jumbled – just like trying to remember events from your childhood. But the more you practise, the clearer it becomes. As you accumulate past life clues, be willing to use your imagination as this will often allow a more accurate picture to unfold.

*

PAST LIFE CLUES

Through analysis of your present strong tendencies you can pretty accurately surmise what kind of life you led before.
Paramahansa Yogananda, MAN'S ETERNAL QUEST

In investigating reincarnation you might find it valuable to begin by exploring your current life for clues that could give indications of past lives. I strongly recommend doing this exercise before advancing to the past life regression process at the end of this chapter. It is an excellent way to explore past lives without requiring you to go into an altered state of consciousness through past life regression. In addition it is a very powerful way to begin to open the door for spontaneous past life recall in your dreams or regressions. You might think of yourself as a 'past life detective' as you amass clues from your affinities and experiences in life.

No single clue can give you all the answers, but if you put the clues together you can begin to piece together the puzzle of who you might have been. As an exercise, go through the following list and write each topic on top of a fresh sheet of paper.

- Childhood games
- Clothing styles
- Architecture
- Food preferences
- Geographical locations
- Climates
- Cultures
- Time periods or historical events
- Déjà vu experiences

- Occupations
- Talents and abilities
- Race and heritage
- Books and movies
- Animals and pets
- Personality traits and mannerisms
- Fears and phobias
- Injuries, diseases and scars
- Dreams

For example, on top of one sheet write: Food Preferences. Then list your food preferences, such as French food and Chinese food. On each sheet write down all the 'clues' that you can gather. Place the completed sheets of paper side by side so that a larger picture can begin to form. For example, when I did this exercise I saw that I had many clues that would indicate a past life in Japan. I've always loved the simple lines of traditional Japanese architecture. In my current life not only did I live for over two years in a Japanese Buddhist monastery, but I studied Japanese culture for two years at university. I have also studied the Japanese tea ceremony and ikebana (Japanese flower arranging), and I have trained in Reiki and Shiatsu, which are Japanese healing systems. My favourite type of restaurant is Japanese. In addition, there was a period in my life when I saw every Samurai movie I could. Toshiro Mifune is a bigger star to me than Robert Redford. Looking at these clues as a 'reincarnation detective', it would make sense that I have lived a life in the Far East.

As you create your list, notice your affinities and experiences and plain 'gut feelings' in each category. For example, under the 'animals' category notice if there is any particular animal towards which you have a close affinity or have always been afraid of. I know a man who has a very close affinity with horses who was a Mongolian in a past life. In that life he loved his horse even more than his wife. In the 'personality traits and mannerisms' category notice any personal mannerisms that you might have. I met a woman who, whenever she is under stress, rubs her throat. In a past life she was stabbed in the throat. Stress was re-enacting a past memory.

Patterns should begin to emerge as you gather your clues together. How will you know if you are accurate? How can you learn to distinguish between simple fascination and a deep stirring of inner knowing? Usually a good indication is your emotional response: it just feels right; there is a gut reaction. If you are unsure, be still for a while and meditate upon the ideas that are beginning to form from your clues. Even if you are not completely clear, sooner or later your subconscious will begin to show you the way to greater understanding. In particular, watch your dreams after you have done this exercise. They should become more vivid with past life images.

Childhood Games

Most common childhood games are the result of programming by society. A little girl might be given a baby doll and told that she is the mother. Her childhood games of playing 'mother' to her babies are, in part, conditioned by her culture. Other childhood games are the result of a child symbolically imitating or 'acting out' adult behaviour around them. A little boy might observe daddy doing repairs about the house. He will then fashion a makeshift hammer and play at making bookshelves. However, sometimes childhood games can be solely a residue of memories from past lives. As you examine the games that you spontaneously played as a child, look out for possible reflections of what could be one of your past lives.

I had a friend who, as a child, used to make a prison-like structure out of cardboard. She then used to get inside her self-created prison and pretend that she was starving. She got her childhood friends to 'sneak' small pieces of dried bread to her. She said that later, when she was as adult, she spontaneously 'remembered' living in a German concentration camp. As soon as she recalled her past life in the camp, she understood why she had played that game over and over again as a child. She was re-enacting a very significant time in a past life.

When I was six I used to go into the woods by our house alone. I spent hours picking small bits of different plants and tasting them. Then I would bring a bunch of my selected plants home. I would let them dry and try to grind them up into a powder. I called my plant mixtures and powders 'medicine'. I would try to get all my friends to have some 'medicine' if they weren't feeling well. I believe that this childhood game was a reflection and a reliving of my memories as a Blackfoot Indian who used to gather herbs for medicine for her tribal people. A sceptic might say that my childhood game of making 'medicine' could have been a result of programming by stories that I might have heard or by information that I subconsciously absorbed. Even if this is so, why did I fixate on one particular piece of information to the exclusion of all others? And how does a sceptic explain a child virtuoso ... a child who is a master musician even though born to non-musical parents? Though it is impossible to prove, beyond a doubt, the fact of reincarnation, it is enormously valuable to observe childhood games for they often hold important keys to understanding past lives.

The younger the child, usually the more potent the past life memories. My grandmother told me that when I was three I used to get very irritated with her because she didn't remember our life together as sisters. She said I would plaintively enquire again and again, 'Don't you remember?' When Meadow, my daughter, was very young, perhaps only two or three, she used to talk about her servants. This was very curious considering that we lived in a very low-key way and often ate our meals sitting on the floor. (This attitude can probably be traced to my Native American life, when I sat on the ground by the fire to eat.) However, even as a two-year-old, Meadow would insist on sitting at the table, placing numerous spoons, forks and knives very neatly next to her plate as if in a formal table setting. She also used to ask me to lay her clothes out on the bed 'because my servants used to lay out my clothes for me'.

When her friends would come to play, Meadow would organize very genteel games with elaborate tea parties. One day her friends went outside to play and I encouraged her to go with them. She responded with such sadness, 'I'm not allowed to play with other children. I'm not allowed to get my clothes soiled.' The pain and sadness of a lonely royal or formal past life filtered through into her childhood games. So many times childhood attitudes can be attributed to environment or upbringing. But not in her case, for my husband and I are roll-up-your-sleeves, down-home kind of people. Meadow continues to be quite the lady. However, I can't help but think that she chose us as parents to balance a past life that may have been formal and rigid.

Clothing Styles

Often a valuable clue to your past lives can be found in the fashion styles to which you are drawn. For example, if your clothing usually includes long, flowing scarves and soft loose fabrics, and you love the tall, stately stone pillars of Greek architecture, you might have had a previous life in ancient Greece. Of course there could be many reasons why you prefer those particular clothes, but as you begin to assemble clues your style preference can be very helpful in understanding the whole picture.

Are you attracted to gypsy-style, peasant-style, military-style, ethnic-style or something else? Do you enjoy wearing long dresses or dinner jackets, or do you loathe formal wear and just like to feel comfortable? Are there any particular styles of hats that you have worn? I knew an American who always wore a Greek cap, and then discovered that he had been a Greek sailor. I came across a Frenchman who continually wore a cowboy hat. He discovered he had lived as a cowboy in the nineteenth-century Wild West. An Australian woman who always wore a beret felt that she had been in the French Resistance during World War II. The colours of your clothing, too, may have past life significance. I knew a woman who always wore clothes in saffron yellow – it was more or less her trade mark.

Regressed to a past life, she recalled being a Hindu monk in India and wearing saffron-coloured robes every day.

Architecture

Examine the architecture styles to which you are attracted. Are you fascinated by Tudor, Georgian or Victorian architecture, or are you interested in structures such as cabins, teepees, yurts, cliff dwellings, castles or Greek temples? What kind of architecture do you like? What kind of architecture do you dislike?

Food Preferences

If you were to pick the type of food that you most enjoyed, would you go for Indian, Chinese, Thai, Japanese, French, Italian, Greek, African, Spanish, Mexican, English, Scandinavian, German, Russian, Vietnamese, Hungarian or some other type of food? Is there a particular food or type of food that you are inclined towards? For example, if you really love pineapples and papayas this might indicate that you lived in a tropical climate. If you are passionate about pickled herring this might indicate a life in Scandinavia. Is there a food to which you are allergic? Food allergies, of course, can come from many sources, but I have had clients who discovered that their food allergy had its source in a past life.

Geographical Locations

Are there countries to which you have been attracted or have always wanted to visit? Perhaps there is a country that you have visited again and again. Is there a country towards which you feel a repulsion and never want to visit? One seminar participant discovered that his lifelong repulsion to travelling to India had its source in an unhappy lifetime in one of that country's northern regions. Do you feel an affinity to a particular kind of landscape, such as mountains, deserts, hills, misty moors, meadowlands, the sea or somewhere else? What is your favourite kind of geographical location? Note down geographical locations that evoke an emotional response, whether positive or negative.

Climates

In what climate do you feel emotionally most comfortable? Do you like dry, arid heat? This might indicate that you lived in a desert environment. Do you like moist, warm tropical climates? Or do you prefer the clean, crisp coolness of winter snow? Imagine yourself in different climates and note your different emotional responses to each.

Cultures

Do certain cultures interest you? Are you fascinated, for instance, by the American Indian culture or Egyptian culture or the Aztec or North African culture? Are there designs or symbols that appeal to you? Look, for example, at those of Celtic, Egyptian, Maori, Native American, African, Chinese, Japanese, Indian, Viking, Roman and Middle Eastern cultures. Do any of these feel familiar to you? Over and over again as a child I used to draw a Star of David. This gives credence to me, among many other clues, that I may have had a Jewish life.

Time Periods or Historical Events

Examine periods in time that have interested you in your present life. Cast your mind back to your school days. Was there a particular period such as the Stone Age, the Bronze Age, the time of the Pharaohs, the Middle Ages, the Renaissance or the Industrial Revolution that appealed to you then? Are there historical events that greatly interest you, such as the Armada, the French Revolution, or World War I? Consult any brief history of the world and see if there are periods that stand out in your mind. Remember, however, that most books of this kind ignore native cultures and you will have to look elsewhere for this type of information.

Déjà Vu Experiences

If you have ever been in a particular place and felt that you had been there before, write that down on your sheet of paper. Note any time when you have met someone and felt that you knew them already. Psychologists say that déjà vu experiences occur when the scene that you are observing becomes available to your conscious mind a split second before you are consciously aware of it. You feel that you have seen the scene before because indeed you have – a split second earlier. However, I have found a direct correlation between déjà vu experiences and past lives. These experiences are very important in your past life exploration. Carefully examine your life, recording all your déjà vu experiences.

I once had a very powerful déjà vu experience that gave me an understanding of one of my past lives. Over twenty years ago I was sightseeing in Venice, and a girlfriend and I decided to hire a gondola to visit some of the neighbouring islands. One particular island seemed to glisten more brightly than the others in the distant haze, and I pointed it out to our gondolier. This beguiling gem in the sea seemed to be beckoning mysteriously to me. Soon we landed at a small jetty.

As I disembarked, a slightly balding, round Franciscan monk came scurrying out to greet us. He spoke some English and offered to give me a tour of the entire island, which was entirely taken up by his monastery and its grounds. As I followed him, I was swept away by an overwhelming feeling of déjà vu. I felt so comfortable on this small island – I knew exactly what lay around each corner even before we reached it. Images and forgotten memories flooded my consciousness. How could it be that I knew my way so clearly? I had never heard of this island before. Suddenly, as we rounded a new corner, I viewed a scene far different from the one I was 'remembering'. Quite spontaneously I exclaimed, 'Oh, this is new!' With an astonished look the monk replied, 'It is new to the original structure . . . but it is more than six hundred years old.' To my amazement, I had unearthed memories of being a monk on this lovely island over six hundred years before.

Occupations

Often the occupations to which we are drawn are duplicates of past life occupations or have similar features. This seems to be especially true of occupations in early life. For example, one man whom I regressed had been a piano-maker in Germany in a past life. In this life, when he was growing up he learned to play the piano and in his twenties he became a carpenter. Both of these occupations are connected with his life as a piano-maker. He is now neither a pianist nor a carpenter, but an artist. I believe that he has completed the karma from that past German life so he is no longer involved in occupations that were similar to that life.

Talents and Abilities

Many of the abilities that come to you spontaneously and easily can be attributed to past lives. Perhaps child prodigies like Mozart, who played the harpsichord with great virtuosity from an early age, gained their abilities from a past life. Examining your spontaneous and natural abilities might give additional clues as to who you were.

One Saturday morning our daughter announced that she wanted to go skating. She had been watching a skating competition on television the evening before and had been enthralled with its beauty and grace. My husband is usually very slow to get going in the morning, so I was astounded when he agreed straightaway – especially since he had never ice skated in his life.

Our experiences when we got to the rink were very different. My daughter had roller skated before but never ice skated. Very quickly her ankles began to wobble and she plopped down on the ice. I had skated a lot as a child but I was rusty and shaky. As I helped Meadow up from the ice we looked for David, the non-skater. Just at that moment he sailed past with smooth, graceful, gliding movements. He turned in circles. He skated backwards. He skated fast. He skated slowly. He completed wondrous spins and turns. Astonishing! Then, after several minutes of pirouetting around the rink, his feet suddenly flew out from under him and he pulled a muscle in his knee. It was as though something inside knew exactly how to skate, but the muscles in his present body weren't prepared to be moved in those directions. Previously he had recalled living in Holland as a burgermeister, a civic official, where he had often skated on canals and frozen ponds. I believe that in his present life his memories of ice skating in Holland had filtered through from his past.

Race and Heritage

I have noticed that there is some correlation between a person's cultural and/or racial heritage and the types of past lives they have had. This correlation is not invariable and to date there has been very little research into this phenomenon. However, a person will often have an ancestor in a culture in which they have a past life experience. A man with a great-grandfather from Germany might discover that he had been German in a previous lifetime, even though he did not regard himself as German in this time.

Books and Films

Pursuing your interest in past lives can be as easy as looking through travel books or the *National Geographic* magazine to observe your reactions to various scenes. Read about different cultures in an encyclopedia and notice which cultures you find interesting. Look at picture books of different environments and notice how they affect you. For example, look at some photographs of desert scenes and see if you have any emotional reactions to them. If you do have an emotional response, take a second step and use your imagination to put yourself in the photograph. Imagine what you might have looked like or what kind of life might have gone along with the photograph.

Note the kinds of books to which you have been attracted during your life. As a child I read every book that I could find about the Amazon. I was fascinated by those steamy jungle scenes and completely entranced by the abundance of wildlife, especially the anacondas. As a child I loved going to the zoo to look at the large snakes and even got my parents to introduce me to a snake expert. I actually got to hold an anaconda and a boa constrictor, which was one of the great thrills of my childhood. I even raised and bred snakes. But there was nothing in my upbringing to have suggested an interest in snakes and the jungle.

Examining the types of books, films and plays that attract you is very valuable in your exploration of past lives. Even if you have read the same bestseller that millions of other people have read, there might be certain scenes that have stuck in your mind that are different from the scenes that have remained in the minds of others. Make a list of the images and scenes in the books you have read and films that you have seen that have particularly impressed you.

Animals and Pets

Do you feel especially drawn to certain kinds of animals? When you are with these animals do you feel you are able to communicate with them? This type of experience may be related to a past life in which you had extensive contact with one particular kind of animal. Perhaps you were a horse trainer or a farmer. Or perhaps, at some point in time, your only friend may have been an animal. The emotional solace provided by that relationship may have been the one thing that kept you going through an incredibly difficult experience. There are accounts of prisoners who formed relationships with rats in their cells, saving a portion of their meagre rations to feed their animal friend. This act of unselfishness, along with the gratitude of the animal, kept them from going insane.

To the ancient Egyptians, cats were gods. The paintings in their tombs are filled with regal pictures of cats acting out their most important myths. In fact, cats were so honoured that many of them were embalmed along with their owners when they died. If you have had a lifelong affinity with cats, to the point of nearly worshipping them, you could have had a life in ancient Egypt.

Personality Traits and Mannerisms

Another set of clues to the past lives you may have led can be found through studying the mannerisms and personality traits which make you unique. Of course, many of these quirks and characteristics can be traced to events and influences in the present life. But often people exhibit certain types of behaviour which would seem on the surface to make no sense in terms of their personal history. For example, a man who is normally very mild-mannered, and who came from a refined and educated family who were kind and never lost their tempers, might find that whenever he witnesses cruelty to children he feels sudden, violent anger and has to restrain himself from acting inappropriately. He may have even wanted to kill someone for shouting at their children. In a past life this man may have been in an orphanage where children were never respected and were sometimes treated cruelly.

Personal mannerisms that are completely out of keeping with what someone knows to be true about their upbringing can also be explained through exploration of past lives. Sometimes, individuals who have come from poverty and become extremely wealthy will report that they always loved luxurious things and that they lived as though they had had them under the worst of conditions. They had refined mannerisms and behaved as though they were royalty. It is likely that these people had experienced privilege in previous lifetimes, and therefore had instinctively known how to act and how to go about recreating these conditions in this lifetime.

Fears and Phobias

Many people cannot explain their fears and phobias even after years of exploration in therapy. This phenomenon can sometimes be unravelled only by working through traumas experienced during past lives. For example, a woman might have such an extreme fear of snakes that it inhibits her ability to do things she would otherwise enjoy. She might be afraid to walk anywhere in the country for fear of seeing a snake. Nightmares about snakes have kept her awake for weeks at a time. Finally, through past life regression, such an individual may discover that she was once lowered into a snake pit as punishment of a petty crime she committed in an ancient and barbarous culture in which she once lived. The subconscious fear that this could happen to her for some small thing she might unwittingly do in this life has haunted her for years, but until she was aware of the original source of her fear she was unable to realize that it could not happen now.

Examining the fears and phobias which we carry around but which do not seem to relate to the facts of our present existence can be a very useful tool for deciphering just what kind of experiences we may have gone through in the lives we lived before this one. Many clients have come to me for help with working on their persistent fears and phobias. This is one of the main reasons why many people choose to do past life work. Fearful experiences in past lives are often re-created in present lives. Thus you will find that whatever you fear will return again and again to your life until you overcome your fear. This is a cosmic law. We recreate similar circumstances in our present life to release blockages from the past. So examine your fears and phobias. You might even imagine possible scenarios that could accompany them so as to gain understanding about who you may have been.

Injuries, Diseases and Scars

In my past life regressions I have found a definite correlation between the injuries, diseases and even scars that we have in this life and what has occurred in other lives. In past life regression a woman vividly remembered having been shot in the forehead. Interestingly this woman found, beneath her hairline, an unusual small indentation that looked as if a small bullet had passed into her head. Another individual developed an incredible blistering rash as a thirteen-year-old. As an adult, during a regression she experienced burning to death in a past life in Spain as a thirteen-year-old servant. When she reached the same age in this life she subconsciously activated a memory of burning to death in another life. Her subconscious association contributed to the development of a rash that resembled burns. In my experience I have found that we often develop physical conditions at a similar age to the onset of that condition in a past life. Even birthmarks can carry clues to past lives. As an exercise you might look at your birthmarks or scars and ask yourself what might have made a mark like that; then notice any images or feelings that well up from within you.

Dreams

One of the most powerful ways to gain understanding of past lives without experiencing a regression is through observing your dreams (see also Chapter 5). Every dream is not only giving you secret messages regarding your current life and relationships but in addition has messages from the past and even the future.

Once you have compiled all your lists of clues, study this information and start to form a picture of just what some of your past life scenarios might be like. This information can be useful for further past life work you might choose to do, and can also provide you with a feeling of security – you can gain some sense of where you will be travelling, without having to feel as if you are just leaping into the dark. In the following sections I shall discuss methods for regression which will take you directly into the past you have been exploring in a tentative way, so that you can acquire an in-focus view of exactly where you have come from.

*

REGRESSION

The most common method of past life regression involves using your powers of visualization. The reason why visualization is an excellent technique is that it allows you to reach the subconscious – and once reached, your subconscious mind cannot tell the difference between a real experience and one that is vividly imagined. It is medically and scientifically recognized that visualized images actually bring about psychological and even physiological changes in some cases to almost the same degree as direct experience.

A study carried out at the University of Chicago demonstrated the power of visualization. A group of college students were divided into three groups and their basketball shooting abilities were noted. The different groups were observed performing a manoeuvre called foul shots; each group underwent a different kind of mental preparation. (Foul shots are when a player stands on a certain line and throws the ball towards a basket hoop. The distance between the basket and the player is always the same, and the action of the game is halted while the player attempts the shot.) Group 1 did not practise foul shots for the thirty days of the experiment, and at the end of that time showed no improvement. Group 2 practised foul shots every day for thirty days and showed a 24 per cent improvement. Group 3 practised foul shots only in their minds for thirty days, and showed an astonishing 23 per cent improvement.

The significance of this phenomenon can be applied to past life therapy. If you visualize a journey to a past life and resolve it, your subconscious will recognize the inner journey that you have taken as a real journey – and recognize the resolve that you have come to as a real resolution.

*

VISUALIZATION TECHNIQUE

Step 1   Enter a Sanctuary

To begin your visual journey to the past I usually suggest that you first become very relaxed (see page 93). Then imagine going to a place in nature. You can either imagine some place that you have actually been where you felt at peace, or it can be an imaginary place. Some people have difficulty visualizing. I suggest that, if you are not visual, you get a 'sense' of being in nature or 'feel' that you are in nature. To do this you might imagine what sounds you are perceiving around you – the singing of birds, the whoosh of faraway waterfalls, the babble of a trickling brook.

Trying to get a sense of what smells and bodily sensations you are experiencing might be a more evocative way of travelling into the woods for some people. Do you smell the dampness of spongy moss under your feet? Does the piercing smell of fresh air and pine trees clear out your head? Can you feel the warmth of the sun penetrate your body as you walk along, or perhaps as you lie stretched out on a smooth, sun-drenched rock?

As you imagine being in nature you will feel peace and safety before going on to your past life regression. You will feel the connection we all share with the earth, the mother of all living things here, and this provides a sense of great comfort for many people. I usually have my client meet their guide at this time (see Chapter 7). This increases the feeling of safety and wellbeing before stepping into the past.

Step 2 Transition Options

Once you have imagined a place in nature, it is important to have a transition between being in nature and stepping into a past life. You will be travelling a long way in terms of time, and also sometimes in terms of distance. You can think of these transition exercises as being a kind of gentle vehicle which will carry you where you want to go, so that you can arrive safe and sound, with a minimum of jet lag and culture shock. It is important to recognize that you need such a mechanism in order to let your mind and body adjust to the suspension of normal time and space.

It is also essential to realize that regression exercises can cause very intense emotions, ranging from exhilaration and joy to terror or intense grief, to surge to the surface. Make sure that regression is a positive experience in your life by making a safe place, emotionally and physically, in which to do it. Pick a time when you are not already overwhelmed by external stresses, and make sure that someone whom you care about and trust is ready to help you process whatever comes up for you, if you feel you might need such assistance. This can be helpful not only for dealing with negative emotions, but also for sorting out the positive ones. There is nothing more valuable for getting a perspective on things and for piecing together a whole picture from fragments of information than a good discussion with a friend.

It is important that you thoroughly familiarize yourself with the resolution techniques described in Chapter 6 before you try out any of these full regression processes. You need to have some ideas for resolving the things you may encounter in your past life experiences in order to avoid the possibility of retraumatizing yourself. You don't just want to relive your previous scenarios – you want to be able to resolve them, or maybe even to rewrite your personal history. So read through the techniques below, and then make sure you've also read Chapter 6 before actually trying any of them out.

It is also helpful to review the section in Chapter 5 on dream sequencing and interpretation (pages 113–116). I have included in this section information which is helpful for interpreting the sometimes confusing jumble of images and time periods that can come up during regression processes. For example, different times in your life may reflect different past lives. Let's say that as a young child you used to play war games. It could be that, as a child, you were working out aspects of a past life in which you had died in battle. Then perhaps, as a teenager, you became very involved in art. This interest might reflect aspects of a lifetime during the Renaissance when you were a painter.

When doing past life processes, you will only become aware of lifetimes that reflect something with which you are dealing in your present life. Whatever lifetime becomes apparent to you will contain either people who figure in your life now, or situations or issues that symbolize circumstances of your present life. The more you practise these process exercises, and the more past life experiences you become aware of and resolve, the more balanced and present you can be in your current life.

Here are several different methods that can help you to make a successful transition, which is the first stage necessary to doing the regression exercises which follow.

☆ Time Tunnel

Leave your sanctuary and walk into a time tunnel. You might count the steps or imagine getting closer and closer until you finally step into a past life.

☆ Bridge of Time

While you are in nature, a bridge appears. You climb up the bridge high above the clouds. As you continue your journey, you descend down the bridge through the clouds into a past life.

☆ River of Time

You step into a small boat lined with soft pillows. You recline on the pillows and watch the clouds overhead while the boat travels of its own volition down the river of time, taking you to a past life.

☆ Lift

Get into the cosmic lift. Every number on the panel of lights in the lift represents a different life. You can either push a button or wait for the lift to stop. When the door opens you step into a past life.

☆ Room of Doors

You enter a circular room with many doors, or walk down a hallway lined with doors on either side. Each door opens to one of your past lives. If you like, you can imagine small windows to look through in each door before you open it.

☆ Time Machine

A time machine appears in your sanctuary. You step in and the time machine lifts up into the clouds. When it descends you are in a past life. You can even have a panel in the time machine that shows you the exact date when you have arrived.

H G Wells !

☆ Mists of Time

Your sanctuary in nature becomes very misty. As you walk into the mists you know that an amazing transition is occurring – your body is going through a metamorphosis. Although you cannot see it happening, you can feel your body change as it becomes the body you occupied in a past life. Then you step into your past life.

There are many variations on the methods described above. Some visualization methods work better for some than others.

*

PAST LIFE PROCESS

To program yourself for past life recall, ask someone to read the following to you in a very soothing voice. You can also tape yourself reading the process and play it back. If you are making a tape recording for yourself, substitute 'I' for 'you'.

Start by getting your body into a very relaxed position, either sitting or reclining. Now take some very deep, relaxed breaths. With each breath you take, you are becoming more and more relaxed. Each breath you take, each sound you hear, allows you to become more and more relaxed.

Now put your attention on your left foot and feel it relax. It is now completely relaxed. Now put your awareness in your right foot and feel it completely let go and relax. Allow that delicious feeling of relaxation to roll up your left leg and just let it relax. Good. Now put your awareness in your right leg and let that same wonderful feeling of relaxation roll up it. Now let your right leg completely relax. Continue to feel a slow wave of relaxation roll up from your feet, through your legs, up your torso, out of your arms and up and out of the top of your head. Your entire body is now relaxed and warm and comfortable. Take one very deep breath and totally relax and let go.

Now imagine you are walking across a field. It's a warm day and you are filled with the full, rich smell of the grass. You hear the gentle drone of insects and the summer songs of birds . . . these sounds fill the air with a soothing, rhythmic cadence. A mist begins to rise up from the fields and a stillness fills the air. In the distance you hear the gentle sounds of a river lapping against the bank. You approach the river. The mists are becoming very thick. As you reach the edge of the river, you notice a sturdy bridge crossing it. The mist has become so thick that you can't see the other side of the bridge. In fact, you can only see a few feet in front of you as you step on to it. With each step you take, you know you are nearing one of your past lives. You are crossing the ever-flowing river of time. I shall count from 1 to 22. When I reach 22 you will step off the bridge at a time far back, before you came into your present body. 1–2–3–4 . . . with each step you take, the swirling, mystical mist seems to embrace you with warmth and love . . . 5–6–7–8–9 . . . you are aware of a very loving presence guiding and protecting your every step. 10–11–12–13–14–15–16–17 . . . the fog is beginning to thin. 18–19 . . . the end of the bridge is near. 20–21–22 . . . step off the bridge.

You have arrived in another time, in one of your past lives. The mist has completely cleared. Look down at your feet. Are they the feet of a man or a woman? Are they young feet or old feet? Are you standing outside or inside? What surface are you standing on? Sand? Stone? Tile? Wooden floor? Grass? What covering do you have on your feet? What clothes do you have on? Look around and note what you perceive. Are you in the country or the city? If there are any buildings, notice the architecture. Are there any people nearby? If there are, listen to them speaking. What language does it sound like? Are there any people that resemble people in your present life? As you explore and perceive this life, notice your feelings and emotions. How does it feel to be in that life? You have a few minutes to explore that life . . . you may do it now.

Now go to a time in that lifetime that was very significant or important to you. You have a short while to experience what is happening and how you feel about these circumstances.

Now go forward in time in the past life that you are exploring . . . go forward to the time when you are about to shed your body and pass over to the spirit world. How did you die? Was it slowly or suddenly? What people were around you? Were you reluctant to go or glad? The process of dying is seldom recognized as a painful event, and there is usually a great sigh of relief once you realize you have passed over. It's like returning home after a long absence. You have a minute to observe this significant event in your past life. You may do this now.

Now go forward into the spirit world. From your perspective in the spirit world, what did you learn from this past life? Were there any fears or concerns from that life that are present in your life today?

As you realize where those fears originated, you know that they are not real and it is simple to release them. Just release them. You know that you can create your life in the present to be exactly the way you want it. You know that you can choose freely without programming from other lives.

Now it is time to let this previous life fade away and return to your present life. Just let that past life fade away . . . just drift away.

As you move more and more towards normal waking awareness, you feel good, strong and empowered. You have stepped into your far past with courage and have looked without judgement at who and what you have been. By this very looking, your present life is enhanced and enriched. By this very observing, you have taken a step closer to the divinity within you. You are free to explore any past life, and the knowledge you gain creates the space for your life to be more fulfilling and whole.

I'm going to count from 1 to 5. When I reach 5, you will be totally awake and aware. 1-2 . . . your body is healthy and strong. 3 . . . more and more awake. 4 . . . your eyes feel as if they have been bathed in fresh, cool spring water. 5 . . . wide awake and feeling great. Open your eyes now. Stretch and enjoy the beauty of the day.

'Follow the Feeling' Technique

Another technique that is valuable to locating a past life is what I call 'follow the feeling'. First begin by locating the area of your life with which you would like assistance. These are some areas that you might consider examining:

- Things you would like to forgive in others
- Things you would like to forgive in yourself
- Health issues
- Fears or phobias
- Talents or strengths you want to reawaken
- Blockages in your life

Step 1   Locate Body Sensation

Identify the issue in your life that you want to work with. Then just relax. Allow yourself to be aware of what emotion or feeling you might associate with your area of concern. Then feel that emotion. To feel emotions, locate where they are causing changes in your body. For example, you might locate fear as a tightening feeling in the centre of your chest, or you could be holding your breath. Now go through your body and locate the area where you can feel the emotion associated with the issue that you want to work on.

An example might be that you are angry with your father for mistreating you during childhood and you want to forgive him. Think about your father and the mistreatment you suffered. Feel the anger. Now travel inside your body in your imagination – find whereabouts in your body you feel the anger. The anger may feel like a lump in your chest. Next focus your entire attention on the centre of your chest and ask yourself what this feeling in your body might look like. Use the following criteria:

- colour
- size
- shape
- texture

To understand how to do this, imagine that you could 'see' feelings inside your body. What colour might they be? Then do this for size, shape and texture. For example, your anger at your father might 'look' oblong and dark blue, about the size of a football, residing in the centre of your chest. Answering these questions helps to activate the stored memories in your body because it focuses attention on it. This is a powerful technique, because every memory is not just lodged in your brain – past life memories are also lodged in your body. Using the body is a very unique way to access past lives.

Step 2   Regress

Keeping your awareness on the particular place in your body that you have chosen, notice any spontaneous memories that surface. Even if the memories that surface are from last week rather than a past life, that's all right. Ask to 'see' an earlier similar memory. We keep recreating similar scenarios lifetime after lifetime. Keep regressing backwards through earlier similar memories until you reach a memory that seems to be the source of your difficulty. At that point you can use any of the resolution techniques described in Chapter 6.

Regression Technique

This is a very simple technique. Allow yourself to become very relaxed and begin to go backwards in time.

Step 1   Recall

- yesterday
- last week
- last month
- last year
- childhood
- into womb
- past life

*

OTHER TECHNIQUES

Look in a Mirror

This is a simple technique. Become very still and relaxed. You might even light a candle. In a partially lit room stare at your reflection in a mirror. Sometimes your face will change shape and you can begin to see how you might have looked in a past life. Periodically close your eyes and see if any images arise spontaneously. Relax. Open your mind to the infinity of the universe, and to the endless possibilities in your own past. If you begin to feel too frightened or disoriented working with this method, take a break and try again later. Or you might want to try a variation of this technique, working one-on-one, as described below.

One-on-One

This technique is similar to the mirror technique described above, except that you do it with a friend. It is important to choose someone you trust deeply, and who can help you process any feelings which may come up.

Working with someone else can be done in one of two ways. You can look into each other's faces and mutually look for clues as to who the other person may have been in another life. Or one person can look at the other, who simply sits still and relaxes. In either case, you will be concentrating on the face of your partner in the same way as you looked at your own face in the mirror exercise. Often you will start to see their face change and they will seem to look different. Sometimes they will look to be a different sex from their present one. Sometimes they will look a different race or a different age. Trust your intuition, and you can gain clues as to who they may have been.

Group Regression

You can go to a seminar where past life regressions are done. Most of my work now is with groups, usually two hundred at a time. I find this very effective because there is a tremendous amount of energy available in a large group. Because the energy is so intense, it is important that the person leading the regression is someone with many years of experience and a person about whom you feel good. It is a good idea to get personal references from people who have previously attended a regression with the therapist who will be leading the group you are considering. At my seminars I would usually have a number of qualified therapists to help the participants if needed.

Tapes

Some people are able to use regression tapes quite successfully. The first time I recorded my regression tapes the sound engineer in the recording studio (who did not believe in past lives) fell off his stool and spontaneously got in touch with a past life. On page 169 there is an address from which you can obtain my past life regression tapes if you are interested.

Past Life Therapist

There are some issues in life that need the help of a therapist. Make sure that you feel good about the therapist with whom you work. Ask around and see who is recommended. One indication that you might need a therapist to help you work through some of the things that can come up for you in regression is if the feelings you are experiencing are interfering with your ability to go about your normal life. If you are feeling completely overwhelmed and cannot cope, get help. It is wise to seek references from someone you trust. You might want to check the certification and credentials of the therapist you choose. When selecting a therapist, understand that, while some painful things may come up which need to be worked through, you should never feel worse overall than you did before you started therapy. Working with the person you choose should bring you a sense of relief, and you must believe that they respect you and that you can trust them at a basic level.

Dreams

A most powerful way to connect with past lives is through your dreams. I feel that this is a very important area and so I have devoted the whole of Chapter 5 to this subject.

These are just a few of the many techniques that can be used to access past lives. In your past life processes, remember that different chronological times in your life will reflect different past lives you have had.

As your present life mirrors different past lives, you will usually be surrounded or closely involved with people from that particular past life. For example, Sarah became very absorbed with her spiritual path and became involved with her local church. She began to assist at the church's Sunday morning children's group and she developed a number of new friendships within the scheme. At the same time in her life she developed a fascination with candles and incense. In a past life regression she discovered that she had been a nun in the south of France (where they had burned many candles and used incense) and found that her new church friends had all been nuns at the same Abbey. In their shared past life they had all cared for orphaned children. They were all drawn together again in similar circumstances to complete any karma they may have accrued together in their past life.

It's also important to remember to have fun in your past life explorations. As you can enjoy the entire process and let go of concerns about being always historically correct, it becomes easier for your subconscious mind to travel into your past life memories. If you are constantly questioning with your critical mind the validity of the historical facts of your past life, you can lose the psychological value of your exploration and it becomes more difficult to recall your past life accurately. It would be as if you were trying to remember your present life birthday party as a twelve year old. If your critical mind kept saying, 'No that can't be right', it would become increasingly difficult to remember your birthday.

IMPORTANT: If you ever feel really 'stuck' or are working on a very difficult life issue, such as abuse, I suggest that you see a therapist who has regression skills. There are many deep issues that respond best under the loving guidance of a therapist.

Through using past life recall exercises you can open the door to the past, and can begin to release limitations from past lives and have a more beautiful loving future. Past life exploration, through waking life exploration and through your dreams, can help you gain an unparalleled understanding of present life circumstances. In the next chapter I have included information on how to program your dreams for past life recall.

5

*

Dreams and Past Lives

The question of karma is obscure to me, as is also the problem of personal rebirth . . . Recently, however, I observed in myself a series of dreams which would seem to describe the process of reincarnation.

C. G. Jung, MEMORIES, DREAMS, REFLECTIONS

*I*t is commonly accepted that dreams can give you potent information about your present. These mysterious messages from your mind can warn you of danger, or they may contain the seeds for creative inspiration. Einstein stated that his theory of relativity came as a result of a dream, and in fact many of his discoveries came as a result of dreams.

In addition, these nocturnal visions can serve as a gateway to the mystic arenas of the night for inner-dimensional travel and communication with the inner realms. They can be a springboard for night healing, astral travel and soul-searching. Dreams can foretell the future and give you valuable information about the past. They are a viable way for your guides to communicate directly with you without going through the censor of your conscious mind. And importantly, dreams can be a door for you to pass through to travel through time and space in order to step into a past life.

D. Scott Rogo of John F. Kennedy University in California did some very interesting research regarding reincarnation memories occurring in dreams. He placed advertisements in metaphysical-oriented magazines to elicit responses from anyone who had experienced past life memories other than through regression. In his book *The Search for Yesterday* Rogo reported that the largest group of credible recollections of past lives came from dreams.

When you are dreaming, your mind is much less likely to be confined by the limits of everyday logic. This accounts for the fact that it is often easier to connect with past lives through your dreams than by any other method. Even people who don't believe in reincarnation will report dreams in which they were participating in activities at another time in history. This can, of course, be attributed to a recently seen movie or a recently read book. However, there are some qualities that distinguish past life dreams from ordinary dreams.

Past life dreams seem much more real than conventional dreams. The colours are brighter. Edges and corners are sharper. Everything seems much more vivid and clear than in ordinary dreams. Frederick Lenz, a psychologist with the New School for Social Research in New York, reports in his book *Lifetimes* that many subjects were aware and very strongly affected when their dreams were of former lives. Often past life dreams will be recurring dreams. Usually in such dreams there is some unresolved issue that is desperately trying to filter through to present consciousness. When these unresolved issues reach the dream state it is an invitation for us to resolve the conflict or difficulty that was left unsolved so long ago. And once this work is accomplished, dreams will often herald the release of old limitations from an accumulation of past lives.

*

DREAMS, PAST LIVES AND THE NEW HARMONICS

I believe that in the next few years there is going to be a huge increase in the number of past life images appearing in dreams. Our dreams are increasingly going to become filtering grounds for past life issues that are influencing our present and struggling to reach resolution.

I like to use a metaphor to explain why our dreams are going to be so important for resolving past life issues. Imagine the midnight darkness of a desert night. The sky is punctuated by exquisite shimmering stars. A celestial canopy radiates above as cars below wind their way along a desert road. Most of the occupants are enjoying the grand beauty of the night. However, a few cars have their radios turned on, but since they are miles away from any radio stations they can't pick up anything. Then, from the farthest reaches of the universe, CRS (COSMIC RADIO STATION) begins to broadcast towards the earth.

Those with their car radios on begin to hear static, as wave after wave of increasingly higher frequencies are projected to our planet. As the intensity of these beams increases the static also increases, until fine tuning brings the signals in clearly. Then all mental and physical tension ease completely. And all those who are listening hear the most exquisite music – music so soothing and beautiful that cares and concerns begin to fade away. The irritations and difficulties in life begin to dissolve and there is a feeling of infinite peace. The very special music from CRS stirs a remembrance in the depths of the soul. Remembrance of a far and distant place . . . a place filled with an abundance of light, of compassion and fulfilment.

Right now, new frequencies and energies are flooding our planet. For many the dreamtime will be like a radio that is turned on. Because of the non-linear intuitive nature of your dreams, you will first 'hear' many of those frequencies through the symbols and images in your dreams. Dreams are an untapped source of enormous potential for the planetary release that is occurring. In the months and years ahead many past life images and symbols will flood your dream state. Those new harmonics will stimulate old blockages that have resided deep within you for lifetimes. Your dreams and your life may feel as if they are filled with 'static'. As these blockages release, you will begin remembering who you truly are and the static will begin to ease, metamorphosing into a beauty you have not known before.

As a child I had the same nightmare night after night. I saw a furnace with an open door. I could see the flames and feel the intense heat. Bodies of adults and children were being put into this furnace. Every morning, I would wake up feeling an abhorrence of what I had experienced in my dreams.

I was very concerned about these dreams. In my early twenties I went to a psychologist who said that my childhood dreams meant I was jealous of my younger brothers and sisters. I was the oldest of four children. She said that as my younger brothers and sisters were born I was consciously helpful and loving. However, subconsciously I wanted to get rid of them or throw them into a furnace. This sounded as though it could have some basis in truth at the time, and as I wasn't having the nightmares any more I was content with her answer.

You hear what you need to hear at any given time in your life. You create what you need at the time. You can't hear things until you are ready.

Last, year, over forty years since my terrifying childhood dreams, I was in London and decided to get a massage. The practitioner was a remarkable human being. I felt that when he worked on me he was not only soothing my body but also reaching into my soul. Abruptly in the middle of the session he looked at me and said, 'You died at Auschwitz.'

I said, 'Excuse me?'

He repeated, 'You died at Auschwitz.'

I replied in shock, 'I don't think that is the kind of thing that I would forget.' (It was also not the sort of thing this man would normally have ever said to anyone, but somehow he felt impelled to say this to me at that moment.)

I explained to him that, as a past life regressionist, I was familiar with my past lives and would not have forgotten a life as monumental as that. Surprised as I was at his revelation, I was also surprised at my own abrupt, almost rude response.

He was very sweet and humble and said, 'All right . . . maybe I was wrong,' and continued to work. But something shook inside me the way a volcano shakes a mountain at its roots. I thought of my recurring nightmare as a child. I thought of how often people had called me a Jewish mother – even though there is no Jewish blood on either side of my family. I thought of the abject terror I felt when I arrived at the German border and had to show my papers before entering the country to give some lectures. I thought of the deep compassion I feel for anyone who is interned unfairly. Amnesty International, a charity which helps those who have been imprisoned unjustly, is a cause about which I feel passionate.

I walked around in a daze. Was I Jewish in my last life? Did I die at Auschwitz? Why don't I remember anything? Why don't I have any visual images? How could I have forgotten that? I didn't talk about my experience. My pride couldn't allow me to conceive that I could have been in Nazi Germany and 'forgotten'. It was too unbelievable.

A few months later, during a break at a seminar I was giving, a man from Holland came and talked to me about growing up in that country during the war. He told me about being a young boy with his mother while they were both interrogated at length. His mother's papers weren't in order, so she was taken away to a prison camp and he never saw her again.

Suddenly, in a voice not seeming to come from me, I said, 'I knew your mother. She was thinking of you before she died. She loved you very, very much.' And we began to sob uncontrollably. I was stunned by what I had said, because I still didn't have any visual memories of being at Auschwitz. Yet something even deeper than visual memories responded to his story. In some place inside me, I knew that I spoke the truth. I was there. I did know his mother. And life had come full circle so that the promise I had made to his mother – to tell her son that his mother loved him until the end – was fulfilled. The vows we make are extraordinarily powerful, transcending time and space.

I was concerned that I still didn't 'remember' having had a past life in a prison camp. But I began to ask friends about their past lives to see if I could gain any further clues as I didn't seem to be able to regress myself. On a subsequent trip to Australia I went out for lunch with a woman who had lived with us for three years in Seattle. She too was a past life regressionist. I enquired, 'You don't ever remember if you had any lifetimes in connection with Nazi Germany?'

She replied, 'Oh, I thought you knew. I was a prison warden at Auschwitz. I've always been fascinated by German culture. I studied German and even lived in Germany as a young woman. In fact, as a child I read *Mein Kampf* nine times!' Suddenly I felt as if I had pulled the handle on the slot machine and won the jackpot.

I remembered that this woman used to wear shiny black boots all the time. And I remember how much I disliked those boots. I began to understand the underlying dynamics of our relationship. I had met her in New Zealand after a severe fall down a cliffside that damaged my spine. Although we barely knew each other, for the weeks that I was on my back she brought me food and took care of me. I could now see that this was re-enacting our life together in Auschwitz where, as a prison guard, she had felt compassion for the prisoners and tried to minister to them. I could understand why I didn't like her black boots. Although she was kind to me in the camp, her boots reminded me of all the Nazi prison wardens.

As I was writing this section I called a very dear family friend who had done extensive regression work to ask him about any connection he might have had with Nazi Germany. He said that when I called him he was reading a book about Auschwitz. He said he definitely remembered having been in a concentration camp. In fact, that very night he was planning a pilgrimage to Auschwitz because he felt that he had some unfinished business which would be helped by going there. I asked if there was anything in his childhood to give credence to the fact that he had been a prisoner in a concentration camp. He stated that when he was a young boy, though he was Christian, he had asked his mother for a Star of David necklace to wear. He remembered his response when asked why he was wearing it: it was so he would never forget the great inhumanity that man had done to man.

My friend also mentioned that when he went to Germany in this life, the instant he crossed over the border his watch stopped, his electric razor didn't work and he developed a rash. When he left Germany his watch and shaver worked again and his rash went away. He too is a very strong advocate of Amnesty

International. In his present life he is a voluntary worker who counsels prisoners; he said he often feels that the prisoners he now works with were the Nazi prison wardens in his past life at Auschwitz. His helping them now is helping him (and them) to heal old emotional wounds.

At different times in our lives different past lives and their associated issues will become prevalent. At this time in my life I am certain I am dealing with issues surrounding my past life in a concentration camp. There is so much more of the puzzle for me to unfold. I still do not have any visual images or memories, but my body's emotional response is so strong that I know I was there.

Currently I am travelling fairly extensively throughout the world. Germany is the only country I visit where attendance at my lectures is limited, and yet I return again and again. It's as if deep inside of me is a yearning to forgive the past completely – the past that I can't quite bring myself to remember.

Dreaming about a past life can allow you to release the blockages during your sleeping hours that are presenting barriers in your waking life. Connecting with your guide during your sleep can assist in past life recall (see Chapter 7). These emissaries of the night can help you open the door to the past.

Before actively pursuing your dreams for information about past lives I suggest that you do the exercise on page 93. After making those preparations, the following steps will allow you to program and stimulate your dreams for past life recall.

Remembering Your Dreams

Science has proved that everyone dreams. In fact, even those individuals who swear that they never dream do so. It's just that they don't remember their dreams. Most dreams only stay in our consciousness for ten minutes. For this reason it is valuable to have a notebook or tape recorder next to your bed so that you can record your dreams immediately before they fade from your memory. Work done by sleep researchers has shown that dreams occur when you are in a very light state at the end of a sleep cycle (a sleep cycle takes ninety minutes). So you don't need to worry about losing sleep by taking time to write down your dreams, because you will be waking at the normal conclusion of a sleep cycle. Keeping a small torch next to your bed does not quite have the shock value of turning on the bedroom light, so you can go back to sleep more easily after noting down the content of your dream.

Remembering your dreams is like any talent. As you practise, you will increase your ability to remember. You might want to date and time your dreams to see if a pattern begins to emerge. For further information about dreams in general, as well as how to remember them, consult my book *Pocketful of Dreams*, (Piatkus Books).

Programming Your Dreams

As you lie down to go to sleep, take a moment to become completely relaxed while at the same time maintaining consciousness. You might begin by slowing down your breath. Take long slow breaths. Inhale completely. Exhale completely. Changing your breath can change your entire bio-electrical system. Changing your breath can change your consciousness.

After you begin to relax you might tell yourself, 'All thoughts, care and concerns are drifting away.' You might imagine that you are standing next to a slow-moving, golden river. One by one imagine taking your cares and placing them on the river in leaf boats. These are the kind of leaf-and-stick boats that a small child might make. Watch each leaf boat gently float away. Watch each and every care and concern just drift away. This allows your mind to be free of interference, so you can become very relaxed.

Then, starting with your toes, go through your body, feeling each part relax. For example, you might breathe into your right foot. Hold your breath for a second. Then, when you exhale, feel your right foot become very relaxed. Continue until your entire body feels completely relaxed. For some people this feels so heavy that they couldn't move if they wanted to. And for some it feels like floating on a cloud.

After you are completely relaxed, make sure that your spine

is straight and then put your awareness in the back of your throat. Imagine a blue light. Keeping your attention on the blue light say to yourself: 'Tonight I travel to one of my past lives . . . and I remember my dreams.' Hold this thought with as much intention as you can while you drift off to sleep.

This is an ancient Tibetan technique – although, interestingly, it could have its basis in scientific fact. Modern science has discovered that dreams originate in the stem of the brain which lies directly behind the back of the throat. Science has also shown that focusing attention on one part of the anatomy increases the blood circulation to that area. So putting your awareness in the back of your throat could increase the blood flow to the area of the brain where dreams originate and thus could cause a heightened awareness of dreaming.

While you are programming your dreams, you might consider concentrating on one particular area of your life that needs assistance and focus on that just before you fall asleep. As you are doing your blue light technique, concentrate on the *feeling* associated with the area that you want to work on in your sleep.

Below are some areas with which you might consider working.

☆ Phobias and Fears

I believe that all phobias and fears that cannot be attributed to this life can be linked to an experience in a past life. When you are going to sleep, pick an area that is posing a problem for you in your everyday life. Are you afraid of confronting your boss to the extent that your working life is nearly unbearable because he/she is always mistreating you? Are you constantly anxious about your health? Take a moment to focus on the physical feelings that this problem manifests in your body. Are you breathing quickly, is your stomach tight, is your throat constricted, or is your head tense and hurting? Just feel the physical sensations connected to your thoughts about the problem. Then, as you do the blue light exercise, imagine that the energy of this light is pervading the part(s) of your body where the most tension is accumulated. Say to yourself, 'Dreams, show me the source of my fear in my past, and lead me to a resolution of all fear.' Hold this intention in the back of your throat as you feel the energy gently infusing your whole body and as you drift off to sleep.

☆ Physical Ailments and Injuries

Many present-day ailments are a reliving of past life injuries or ailments. Sometimes our current physical challenges can also be symbolic of past life trauma. For example, someone who has breathing problems may have had a past life where they suffocated to death. Or a person with chronic back pain may have had a life in which they felt they could never stand up for themselves.

As I have described above, in the section on fears, place your awareness on the physical feelings in your body associated with whatever ailments are preventing you from having a sense of total wellbeing. If there are many problems and the feelings are overwhelming, just choose the most intense one. Stay with this feeling for a moment, and then imagine the blue light energy gently entering this part of your body, bringing healing and relief. Say to yourself, 'Dreams, reveal to me the source of my discomfort and ailments. Take me back to the time when I first experienced this problem.' Hold on to this thought. Place it in the back of your throat, in the midst of the blue light, and gently go to sleep.

☆ Relationship Difficulties

The people to whom you are very close to or the people with whom you have great difficulty are most likely people who have been important to you in other lifetimes (see the section on soulmates in Chapter 2). Remembering the dynamics of previous relationships in other lifetimes, and seeing how their significance is still affecting the way you relate to people in the here and now, can allow you to explore completely different ways of being with others. To program your dreams for remembrance of these issues, follow the steps described above for dealing with fears and physical ailments. Allow yourself physically to experience the bodily sensations associated with your difficult relationships. When you are not getting along with someone close to you, what parts of your body are affected? Feel that.

And say to yourself, 'My dreams will allow me to remember the significance of this relationship to me in another lifetime, and they will lead me to a wonderful and fulfilling resolution of this issue in my life now.'

☆ Blockages to Creativity and Abundance

Many people create a climate of deprivation for themselves out of a sense of guilt, or a feeling that they shouldn't have the good things in life. Often these feelings seemingly have no relation to the present circumstances of a person's life. Perhaps you are living your life the best way you can, and have no conscious memories of any nagging guilt, but you just can't get over the feeling that you don't deserve to have the things you want. Feeling this way leads to a continual poverty consciousness, which prevents you from manifesting abundance in all aspects of your life. Going back into the past and locating the source of your feelings of unworthiness can free you from the circle of lack and deprivation which you would otherwise feel compelled to continue. In addition to programming your dreams to release the original past life trauma, here is an exercise you can do in conjunction with your past life dream work.

Instead of centring on the feelings associated with the difficulty you are having, you can focus on the desired results. For example, if you are having problems with money, focus on the feelings that you would have if abundance wasn't an issue for you. As you are lying in bed, form a clear picture of the material things you would like to have, where you would like to travel, or whatever circumstances you deeply desire in order to enjoy your life more fully. Just relax and let your mind play in forming these pictures. Enjoy the sights and sounds and smells associated with the things you are desiring. Then say to yourself, 'Tonight when I am sleeping, I will remember where and when I first came to believe that I could not have all that I desire and deserve. Tonight, my dreams will help me to resolve my problems concerning money.'

Let this resolve be filled with the pleasure of the pictures of all the wonderful things you have just been imagining, and don't weigh yourself down with fear and anxiety about everything you feel is currently lacking. Let yourself slip off to sleep, secure in the knowledge that these issues will be resolved, and that the things you wish for are already in the process of becoming part of your reality. Hold your intention lightly and joyously in the back of your throat as you do the blue light exercise.

Writing Your Dreams

As soon as you've had your dream, *immediately* write down what you remember, however insignificant it seems. When you first begin to enter into past lives in your dreams, you might find just an object or two that seem to be from a past life. Past life fragments get woven into dreams that seem to be concerned with purely present life issues. For example, you might be zooming down a motorway in a red sports car, looking out of the window, when you see someone dressed in seventeenth-century clothes. It's as if there is a semi-permeable membrane between this life and other lives. Often, at first, just an object or two from a past life will make it through the membrane into your current dream. As you become more adroit with your dream states, inner-dimensional portals will be made available so that whole scenes or parts of whole scenes will seep through into the present dimension. Eventually you will be able to step through a time-traveller's portal so that you are completely immersed in a past life. Until that time write down anything and everything that you dream. I believe that even the most ordinary of dreams have past life clues woven into them.

Analysing Your Dreams

See if there is any similarity between that dream lifetime period and your current life. Are there people in that life who strike you as similar to someone in your current life? Notice your emotions in that life; notice any decisions or judgements that you made. Are any patterns or habits or fears in that past life present in this one? Perhaps you dream of being lost in the snow and are frightened. In your present life you always avoid any activity that has to do with snow. This might be a clue to having been lost in the snow in a past life. Remember: one clue isn't enough. You must become a 'reincarnation detective' and put all the clues together to get a clear picture of your past.

Make a list of all the major objects in your dreams. The different parts or themes of your dream represent different aspects of you and your life, but they can also signify events or objects from past lives. For example, I had a dream that I was in a building with small rooms. Many people were crowded into those rooms and there was a pervading feeling of fear, of not feeling safe. The major themes here would be (1) small rooms, (2) crowding, and (3) not feeling safe. I listed these important aspects of the dream. The next step was to look for some correlation in my present life.

At present we have builders in our home and the contents of a number of rooms are crowded into just a few. In my life right now I've got a general feeling of being very crowded. In addition, because of the building work some of the doors are off their hinges, and subconsciously, perhaps, I feel that our home isn't very safe. This is a reasonable explanation for my dream. However, yesterday I went to see the film *Schindler's List* that contained a sequence about Auschwitz. I was astonished to see that the crowded rooms that I had dreamed of only nights before looked almost exactly like the rooms in the Warsaw ghetto into which many Jews were crowded before they were sent to the concentration camps. My dream had a correlation with my present life, but at the same time it provided another clue for me as I continue to explore a probable lifetime during which I was interned in Auschwitz.

Some people have past lives appearing very visually and specifically in their dreams. However, not everyone is particularly visual. Some people wake up with no visual images, but they will have a feeling. If you have programmed your dreams for past life recall and you waken with no specific images, take a moment to notice what you are *feeling*. Maybe you are feeling a little sad. Take a moment to expand that sadness into a story. It might go like this: 'This sadness feels like the kind of sadness that one would feel if they lost someone very close to them, perhaps a child. It doesn't feel like my child, but someone else's child. The child was very carefree and happy. I wished I could have warned this child not to get too close to the waterfall.' When you 'make up' your story don't be overly concerned that it is right. The more that you struggle to be *right* the more difficult it is for the images to just flow from your subconscious.

Write down your 'stories' as well as the memories of your dreams. Sometimes the stories seem to have a life of their own and take shape without any effort. It is very important however to do this exercise just as you are waking up. This is the most potent time for your subconscious to give you information about your past. Often people tell me looking at their dream journal records of the 'stories' that have come to them in early morning in addition to their dream memories has allowed the pieces of the reincarnation puzzle to begin to fall into place.

Dream Sequencing and Interpretation

Another technique that you can use for understanding a past life connection in your dreams is to continue your dream once you are awake. I call this technique 'dream sequencing'. You need to set aside twenty to thirty minutes, at any time of day. Find a comfortable chair or bed to recline in and make sure that you won't be disturbed. Take a few minutes to relax completely. You can either deepen your breathing or visualize a pleasant scene. Once you are relaxed, go back into the dream that you recall from the previous night. Even if it is just a wisp of a dream, it will work for this exercise. Now replay the dream, just allowing the dream images to evolve. Don't consciously 'try' to direct the outcome of the scene that is unfolding. Just allow your imagination to roam freely. A 'sequence' is being formed for your dream.

Don't be concerned if some of the things occurring in the dream sequence don't seem to make sense – for instance, if a sixteenth-century queen has a crown made of Tupperware. Remember that the language of dreams is symbolic. Your sleeping mind is an artist weaving together a rich tapestry of images – mixing a bit of this with a bit of that. This is the way it communicates. The subconscious has much more in common with a poet than with an accountant, and in order to understand its language you have to let go of your need for everything to fit together in a logical way. Just try to get the *feel* of what the images evoke for you.

Keep allowing the dream sequence to unfold. If at any time you encounter something uncomfortable you can surround yourself in an imaginary bubble of safety, or you can change the series of events so that the sequence has a resolved outcome.

Often people, things and places in dreams have symbolic significance. This is as true for past life dreams as for dreams that are connected mostly with your present life. Jung and other researchers studied the amazing number of universal symbols which people all over the world recognize and employ in their art and religion, and which show up in their dreams; these are usually known as archetypal symbols. If you see someone famous in your dream sequence, you might of course have known him or her in another life; but more often the famous person represents an archetypal symbol. Let's say Geronimo appears in your dream sequence. It would be likely that he represents that part of you that is 'strength against all odds'.

Because the human mind is such a weaver of symbols, it can be a challenging task to sift out the content of dreams which is related to your present life from those things which are clearly from a past life. Additionally, some people and things appear in dreams literally, as themselves, while others act as symbols for something or someone else. I think the important thing here is to trust your instincts. Your feelings are the best guide to determining what the meaning of the dream is for you. Does the antique chest that looks just like your grandmother's feel as if it has something to do with your family in your present life, or does your heart tell you that it is pointing you in an entirely different direction? I talked about sorting out these different aspects of a dream when I described my dream about the small, crowded rooms.

When you've completed your dream sequence, write it down in a journal. Add it to the clues that you are accumulating. For additional information about analyzing your dreams, please refer to my book *Pocketful of Dreams*.

Resolving Your Dreams

To resolve the issues that are arising in your dream states from past lives it is valuable to imagine that you are going back into your dream. Go back to it immediately, especially if it was a traumatic dream. Now relive the dream; you can feel it fully, detach yourself from it, or change the outcome (see Chapter 6). Resolve the dream in a similar way to resolving an incident in a past life regression.

Change those dream images until you have created a positive outcome in your mind. There is a place inside you that does not recognize the difference between what you experience in your imagination and what you experience in reality. In fact, when you are dreaming, the small muscle groups in your body are reacting as if the event that you are dreaming about is actually taking place. When you dream that you are running, the large muscle groups in your body are paralysed. However, your respiration increases, your heartbeat increases and the small muscle groups respond as if you were actually running. This lends credence to the belief that the images experienced in your mind are recognized by your brain as 'real'. So if you can recreate the images in your dreams to give a positive outcome, you can alter limiting beliefs that have carried over from a past life. It is very exciting that we have such opportunities available to us during our night hours.

*

DREAM PROCESS

This dream process is based on ancient dream techniques. It is safe and easy, and should be done just before sleep. You can record this meditation on a tape, to be played back to yourself before you go to bed. Speak with a very slow, relaxed voice. You might want to include some background music. Remember how important it is to have a pen and paper next to your bed to record your dreams.

To begin this process allow your body to assume a restful position, making sure your spine is straight. You may do this now. Good.

Now begin to take very easy, deep breaths . . . nice and easy breaths. Inhale and exhale. That's good. It's almost as if you yourself are being breathed in and out. It's as if nothing else exists except for your breath. In and out. All your thoughts and cares are drifting away as you continue to breathe in and out. With each breath, you find yourself relaxing more and more. You find yourself moving deeper and deeper within yourself. Imagine that you are flowing into your body as you inhale – and out of your body as you exhale. In and out. Each breath takes you deeper. It is as if you are drifting and flowing with the very gentle ebbing and flowing of the universe and your breath is connecting you to that rhythm, that harmony. Breathe gently and evenly as you continue your journey into a very relaxed, yet aware, state. Allow your awareness to drift gently into your body and allow yourself to be aware of any tightness. Just notice it. Good.

Feel that tightness just melting away like ice melting on a warm summer afternoon. That's good. Drifting and floating. Drifting and floating. Now allow your imagination to begin to drift and float. Just imagine, in your mind's eye, a moonlit night. There's a beautiful full moon and you are walking along the sandy seashore. Ahead, washed in moonlight, is a sumptuous bed. It is luxurious and voluptuous. The pillows are soft and round and firm. Take some time to imagine this bed, making it as real as possible. Make it your perfect bed. Really imagine this bed.

Now, slowly and ever so sensuously, crawl into this bed. Be aware of the opulent plumpness of the pillows. Feel the silky smoothness of the sheets as you slide easily beneath them. It feels so good to be in this bed. Fanned by the gentle sounds of the cadence of the sea, as the tides ebb and flow, you find yourself drifting off into a deeeep, deeeep sleeeep.

Now put your awareness in your present body. Feel the way the sheets feel on your body. Be aware of your head on your pillow. Allow yourself to be aware of the sounds of the night. Listen to the sounds of your own body. As you listen to the sound of your own breath, know that tonight is a special night. Somewhere in the magic of the night, a metamorphosis will occur. You know that you will be gently transported back to another place . . . another time. You will be taken back to one of your past lives. You know that a door to the past will make itself evident in your dreams. As your body sleeps, your spirit will travel through time and space, dancing through the stars and touching past incarnations.

Now imagine that you are going forward in time to the time when you are about to wake up. Your dreams are still very evident. Imagine that, without losing those dream images, you are rolling over and writing those dreams down – dreams that hold the key to your past life.

You may now put your consciousness back into your present body and either return to conscious awareness or drift off to sleep.

You can repeat these exercises again and again. I wish you well on your inner journeys.

6

*

Resolutions: How to Heal Past Life Blockages During Regression

O nce you have entered into a past life, whether in your dreams or in waking life, it is not uncommon to discover something uncomfortable that needs resolution. One of the main benefits of doing past life regression is that you can finally be free of the hindrances that have been blocking the realization of your potential through many lifetimes. However, you will need to learn some techniques for accomplishing this. I shall describe a number of simple exercises that you can do alone or with someone with whom you feel safe. Be sure to seek professional help if you feel it might be helpful. Here are a number of options that can be employed. You might want to try several or all of them to find out what works best for you.

*

FEEL IT

Some people will say, 'What if I do the processes and come up with a lifetime that is scary – or I have a past life nightmare?' Instead of shutting down on those emotions, *choose* to feel them. When you do this, the fear will dissipate. For example, when you go to a cinema to see a horror movie, you have paid money to be scared. You have gone out of your way to create a scary experience for yourself. When you have paid the attendant for the roller coaster ride and you are absolutely terrified – screaming crazily throughout the ride – remember it was *you* who rushed to join the queue.

Don't be afraid of the emotions that you might feel when you get in touch with a past life in your dreams or in waking consciousness. No one would go to hear a symphony if there were only going to be one note played. A symphony needs to have thousands of notes – high points and low points, crescendos and dénouements. Life is like that – enjoy your emotions, the high points and the low points. Each of your emotions is like a precious note in a symphony. As you experience a past life, relish and explore each emotion that arises.

If you find yourself stuck in an emotion, don't deny it or try to get rid of it but move towards it and let it embrace you. See yourself turning round and letting it flow all round you. Make it more. For example, if you discover a lifetime where you were devastated by the death of your lover, instead of trying not to feel that sadness and repressing it – which is what you did at the time – let yourself feel even more sad.

Go into the centre of that sadness and feel it. Find whereabouts in your body that sadness dwells, and allow yourself to feel those sensations even more. This will let you start to release any decisions that have been creating barriers for you.

The emotions that you repress stay with you lifetime after lifetime and create blockages in your life, so it's important to experience your emotions. However, there is a difference between *dramatizing* your emotions and *experiencing* your emotions. When I began doing past life therapy seminars many people during the processes began crying or sobbing sometimes very dramatically. I assumed this was in large part important to the ultimate positive results that they achieved. However, I did a past life seminar in Vancouver, Canada and nobody cried uncontrollably. I was distraught because I assumed that the seminar didn't work and that no one would get results. I was then astonished to receive numerous letters about the results that were being achieved in the lives of the participants of that particular seminar. I assumed it was a fluke but my next seminar was in Toronto and the same thing occurred and has occurred ever since. Very few people become emotionally fraught yet very dramatic positive results are reported. In fact the results were much more dramatic than when everyone experienced catharsis in the seminar. As I began to investigate this phenomenon I realized that instead of externalizing and dramatizing their emotions, they were going to the source of their emotions and truly feeling them. Sometimes dramatizing emotions can, in fact, keep you separate from your emotions. I met a woman who had been crying hard almost everyday for twenty years over the death of her husband. When she went inside her body and went to the source of her sadness she was able to truly grieve for the first time in twenty years. She then 'experienced' her grief instead of externalizing it and was able to completely release her sadness. By finding where in the body the emotion exists and going into the emotion you can release it from its roots.

Here is an exercise that you can do if you begin to feel any uncomfortable emotions during your past life regressions. It is similar to the exercise called Locate Body Sensation in Chapter 4 although that exercise is aimed at recalling a past life. This exercise allows you to release emotions once they have occurred during your past life recall.

Begin by travelling through your body. The way that you know that you have an emotion is because you have a sensation in your body associated with that emotion. For example, your chest might feel constricted during sadness and your shoulders might tighten during anger. It may surprise you to know that not everyone associates the same body sensations with the same emotions.

Once you have located the emotion you are feeling in the body then focus your entire attention on that part of the body and *intensify* the body sensation that you are experiencing. For example, if you are feeling a constriction in the chest, expand that feeling of chest constriction. Feel it more. Usually when we feel an emotion we do everything that we can to suppress the feelings associated with the emotion. This, in fact, adheres the emotion to the body because what you resist ... persists. So the more you *resist* feeling your emotions the more your negative emotions control your life and the more they *persist* in your bio-energy matrix. Dramatizing emotions and catharsis isn't necessarily 'feeling' emotions, so focus your entire attention on the sensations in your body.

As you focus your attention on the particular sensation in your body associated with an emotion, notice what shape the emotion/sensation seems to be. For example, the constriction in the chest associated with sadness might seem to be in a pear shape with the smaller end of the 'pear' pointing down. As you are continuing to focus your attention in your chest notice how big the sensation is. The 'pear' might seem to be about 6 inches wide and 8 inches long. Then notice if the 'pear' had a colour, what colour might it be? (It is not an accident that people associate colour with emotions, i.e. 'She's in the "pink".' 'He's feeling "blue".' 'I'm having a "black" day.' 'He saw "red".')

Continue to ask yourself these questions.

• What body sensation am I feeling that is associated with this emotion? (Sometimes the body sensation will shift to another spot in the body. Follow the sensation where ever it goes.)
• If the sensation had a shape, what shape would it be?
• If the sensation had a size, what size would it be?
• If the sensation had a colour, what colour would it be?

Continue to intensify what you are feeling. Often the colour, shape, size and location change as you are doing this ... just continue to move into your emotions. Often doing this exercise alone is enough to begin to release the uncomfortable emotions that arose during your past life experience. Sometimes spontaneously while you do this exercise, memories from another past life will emerge. These memories will usually contain early similar memories. Just as a temper thrown at age twenty may be the result of a temper tantrum thrown under similar circumstances at age three, so the past life trauma that you are working with may have its source in an early similar lifetime. So don't be surprised if you find yourself catapulted to another lifetime. It is good because you are going to the source of your present day difficulty.

*

DETACH FROM IT

If your find yourself in a situation that holds very uncomfortable emotions, imagine that you are floating above the scene. Just observe it. Detach yourself from the particular view that you held at the time. A technique that I often suggest is to play the incident through at high speed, like an old Charlie Chaplin film. And then have the incident run backwards at high speed. So, if you find yourself running and falling off a cliff, see yourself running and falling very fast and then see yourself flipping up off the ground, soaring back to the top of the cliff, and then running backwards! This exercise can begin to take some of the emotional trauma out of the event and will allow you to detach from it.

When you detach from a situation, it allows you to observe the situation from a wiser perspective than your very limited subjective perspective. Beryl experienced a lifetime where she lost her husband who died of an infection that he got while working in their garden. In her regression she felt tremendous sadness tinged with guilt over her loss. The sadness was for the loss of her husband and the guilt was for the fact that she had been capable of digging the garden but told her husband she wasn't strong enough to do it. Though, of course, it was not her fault, she felt guilty and the guilt had permeated her present life. When she detached from the scene and floated above it to gain an expanded perspective, she saw that her intense love for her husband was sometimes to the detriment of her children. She often abandoned her children's needs to be with her husband. After the death of her husband she began to nurture her children more and give them the attention and love that they needed so that they grew to become fulfilled adults. When she detached from the scene she was able to come to a peace about her husband's death and come to the understanding that everything has a purpose even if we don't understand it at the time.

When you detach from a scene you can float above it or you can watch it as if you were watching a play or a film. If it is very traumatic you can watch yourself watching the scene as a way of further detaching yourself from the situation.

Detaching from a past life scene can allow you to understand that every lifetime, every experience you have, allows you to grow . . . and every experience is important for your evolution as a soul. I believe that Spirit is not so much interested in your comfort as in your personal growth even if it means going through difficult experiences, even if it means breaking an arm or losing a husband. The bottom line that generates your experiences is what can facilitate the greatest growth for you.

Another way to detach from an uncomfortable past life is to make it seem silly. A client came to me who had always felt intimidated by men. She was a mature, responsible woman, but as soon as she was near a man she began to act in a meek, childlike way. She regressed to a life in which she had a very strict, disciplinarian father. She could see that whenever she was with men she activated the memory of being a meek little girl from a past life. In her past life exploration she arrived at a point where her father was giving her a very stern dressing-down. I told her to imagine him standing in front of her in red spotted underpants and with a silly hat on his head. Then she should imagine people walking by and laughing. Suddenly she too was laughing, and she was no longer a meek little girl. This session completely changed her attitude to men.

*

CHANGE IT

I find the most powerful technique to resolve an uncomfortable past life memory is to change the circumstances of your past life until it feels comfortable or enjoyable. I believe that you can actually change the past; but if this is too much for you to accept, then imagine that you are changing the images that are stirred in your brain. As you change those stored images in your brain, imagine you are changing the associated limiting beliefs.

Remember the example of the young man whose friends chased him into the ravine when they thought he was ridiculing the King? Imagine that he changes this past life memory. He stops running and stands his ground. Those who were chasing him stop. There's a stand-off. Then everyone bursts out laughing. Changing his mental image of being hurt for speaking his mind changes the inner belief that he had developed, which says, 'If I say what I really feel, I'll be hurt.' When his limiting belief changes, his life changes. For a man who feels that, if he speaks the truth he will be punished, he will create circumstances to validate this subconscious belief. Physical matter coalesces around us based on our subconscious beliefs. Change your subconscious beliefs, and the world around you will seem to change.

Here is an example from a letter that was sent to me after a past life seminar. It shows the power of changing your past life memories.

I would like to share with you, Denise, a past life that I became aware of during your weekend past life workshop which had an enormous impact on my life now. In this life my son was born with the umbilical cord around his neck and has always been a screamer. He also had a speech pattern that meant he would repeat several words in the sentence many times. He is now three and a half years old and an example of his type of speech is as follows: 'The cat, cat, cat, cat is running running very, very, very, very fast fast.'

The past life I experienced in your 'Journeys into Past Lives Seminar' was a life where my son and I both were American Indians. I was my son's mother and he was about eleven years old. My son and I were separated from our tribe and we were attacked by another tribe. [In the past life regression] I was facing several of the attackers. It became clear to me that they were going to kill me and torture my son. I became very angry and tried to convince them to leave my son alone. When it became clear that this wasn't working, I turned to my son and we both looked deeply into each other's eyes. My son, in an instant, understood what I was going to do, we both screamed and I strangled him.

I don't know why but I wasn't killed and I lived the rest of my lifetime with the anguish of having killed my son. During the regression, I changed the outcome (as you suggested). I saw many images of beautiful crystals and total safety and wonderful open, clear communication between us. For me this was very exciting.

It became even more exciting when I returned to pick up my son from my mother's and she proceeded to tell me that at one point during the weekend my son had gone into the bedroom and begun to sob and sob. The sobbing continued for nearly thirty minutes . . . he couldn't seem to stop. This happened at the exact same time as I was getting in touch with our life together as Indians.

I am writing this just one week later and my son has stopped the word repetitions in his sentences and his screaming has subsided. I used to be so wound up by his screaming that I wanted to put my hands around his neck. Although I never did, the urge to do so was very strong – almost overwhelming.

This regression has been a major turning point for both my son and myself. I feel really excited and empowered as a result of the weekend. Thank you for a most special weekend.

By changing the circumstances of a past life that she and her son were reliving again and again, not only did it change the way that she felt about her son but it also changed his behaviour as well!

Here is another letter sent to me that shows the value of changing the circumstances of a traumatic past life.

Dear Denise,

I was one of the several hundred people at your Past Life Seminar in Sydney in November. You may remember me as the woman who gave you a book during the seminar. My reason for writing is` to tell you about the incredible occurrences that have happened over the last few days since your seminar.

When my husband and his first wife divorced eleven years ago it was very bitter and he was stopped from seeing his children, in particular the youngest child who was seven years old at the time. My husband is a very special person and this has been hard on him.

During one of the weekend's regressions, I concentrated on the thought that if I had been a part of my husband's previous family in a past life, I wanted some insight and understanding. Well, I'm still not sure exactly what my role was in the past life that I experienced except that I saw that I was comforting an old man who was dying. He wasn't dying of old age but of a broken heart, blaming himself for the death by drowning of his three children. I saw that the old man was my present day husband. You told us we could change what was upsetting so I changed the situation. It was in the future in that life and *I* was dying and the old man and his three children were comforting me. They were very close and very happy. This apparently had an effect on the present! Today the youngest child, seemingly out of the clear blue, called and is coming to visit tomorrow. This is the most hopeful thing to have occurred in eleven years! Last night I told my husband of the regression and though he is sceptical, he is open minded. Wow! So thank you, Denise Isn't life grand when you know that love is all that matters?

This example shows that even if you aren't aware of all the details of your past life just by changing the circumstances it can have a very empowering effect on life.

Here is an example from my life that shows step-by-step the mechanics of how to change past life memories.

When my daughter, Meadow, was younger I asked her if I could try a new relaxation technique on her before I tried it on my clients. I needed to hold her wrist, but as I did so she said, 'Mum, you know I don't like to have my wrists touched. In fact I can't even look at my wrists because when I can see the veins I get squeamish.' I hadn't been aware of this before, but proceeded with the relaxation process.

While she was relaxed I thought I would take the opportunity to see if I could get to the source of her difficulty. I said, 'Imagine a situation that might relate to your wrists.' (Children, incidentally, are very easy to regress into past lives. Adults develop a buffering to their intuition so that they usually find it more difficult to be regressed.)

'Mum, I see a desert. I live in the desert.'

I asked her, 'Are you male or female?'

'I'm a young man. I have a religious belief that I feel very strongly about. It's a good belief. I want to tell everyone about it. I know it will help them. I'm now in a small village to tell everyone about this new belief. They don't want to know about it. In fact they are getting very angry. Oh, no.'

'What is it?'

'They're tying me up. They've cut my wrists. I'm watching the blood slowly flow out of my body. I'm tied up so I can't stop it.'

'You can change this experience,' I told her. 'You can replay it but give it a positive outcome.'

'OK. I'm replaying it. . . . I have travelled across the desert to tell the villagers about my new religion. Everyone who greets me is happy to meet me. Everyone seems really interested in talking to me and finding out about my beliefs. When I leave the village I've made many good friends.'

'How do you feel?'

'I feel great. It feels good to know that I can really tell people how I feel.'

All this occurred in about twenty minutes. My daughter came back from her experience feeling refreshed and rejuvenated. I asked her to look at the veins on her wrist. She said she was amazed because she could now look at them without feeling queasy.

Up until that point she had always been very hesitant to say how she truly felt about anything. But now a remarkable thing occurred: she began to tell people how she felt, to share her personal point of view. The Gulf War broke out soon afterwards and Meadow called the fifty students in her class to ask them to march against the war with her. Some students agreed with her, while others vehemently disagreed. The war was something that she felt strongly about, and she was willing to let other people know how she felt. To me, this was a minor miracle. I believe that our one twenty minute session made all the difference.

Some people are concerned that if they change the past then maybe they will be negatively affecting the present. They'll ask, 'What if I change the past and then my mother never meets my father. Will I cease to exist?' Though these kind of questions are interesting to me philosophically, in practicality I find that changing a traumatic past life always has a positive effect on everyone. It seems to me that when you clear an emotional blockage from your energy field this creates a resonance that positively and deeply affects others as well. I believe that you *can* change the past. Even if I am proved wrong and you are not actually changing the past, just changing the images in your brain associated with limiting beliefs has a positive and empowering effect on life.

✶

SEE IT FROM ANOTHER VIEWPOINT

Another technique for resolving a past life situation is to imagine that you are jumping into the awareness or the body of someone else who is present. See the entire situation from their point of view. Almost always when you do this you forgive the actions of others because you recognize that if you were in their place you would react in the same way.

Although I definitely don't condone the actions of the man who shot me, it was enormously helpful for me to imagine that

I was in his consciousness. I felt that he almost couldn't help himself from killing people, in the same way an alcoholic has great difficulty resisting another drink. Sensing reality through his eyes made it much easier for me to forgive him. This was valuable for me, because resentment was eating away at me.

Another interesting example is the case of Charles. Charles had been quarrelling with his younger brother seemingly almost since his brother was born. The quarrelling continued into adulthood and their arguments were having a negative effect on the entire family as each brother tried to get other family members to agree with their point of view. Charles became aware that these altercations were becoming increasingly non-productive and affecting many areas of his life. He attended a past life workshop I gave in New Zealand and during a regression session recalled a past life where he had been an accounting clerk in Denmark and his present day brother had been his demanding and argumentative employer. In the regression he took my suggestion of seeing the scene from another's point of view. He imagined that he was seeing the world through his employer's eyes. Instantly he understood that his former employer had a very severe back pain which made his every move painful. Because of his severe pain he was continually in a foul mood and treated his employees very badly.

Charles understood that his employer couldn't help the way he was acting because his moods were so severely affected by his continuous pain. Charles then began to have compassion and understanding for his employer/brother. (It's interesting to note that his brother in his present life had a back injury.) Charles reported seeing his brother a few days after the seminar and he was astonished to find that there was much less animosity between them and their relationship has continued to grow closer.

Working through past life blockages is one of the most rewarding kinds of work you can do. Many clients have reported a greater sense of exhilaration and joy than they had ever experienced before. But it can be a rough and rocky road while you are still in the process. Share your pain with someone who cares about you, or seek professional help if you think you should, and know that what awaits you on the other side is more than worth it. Freed of the blockages and bindings that until now have been keeping you down, you will finally be able to soar to the heights you have always dreamed of!

7

*

Spirit Guides,
Angels and
Past Lives

*E*veryone has guides, whether he knows it or not, and those who consciously communicate with their guides have an enormous wealth of resources to tap into. Guides come to us from the world of Spirit. They hold a unique perspective of the universe, creation, life and eternal love. Non-physical beings or entities that give guidance, assistance and love, they can be teachers or protectors as well as helping to direct our paths and to release old past life karma. They remind us of the world beyond the 'here and now'. Guides can be of great value in gaining access to your past lives.

People may have multiple guides over a lifetime. Guides may enter and leave our critical life passages, or stay with us consistently over a long period. Guides have their own personalities, their own goals, their own perspective and their own styles of communication. Each person's experience will be different. A guide may appear in the quiet of meditation or arrive as an unseen, loving presence that you feel around yourself as you go about your everyday activities. A guide may appear to you in a daydream, or in a dream at night – as a person dressed in period clothes, or an animal. A guide can arrive as a feeling, a smell, a light, a sound, or even just a 'knowing' that it is present.

My own belief is that guides are actual spiritual beings who exist on higher planes of consciousness and are working to help us in our evolution. Your guides are usually beings who have been with you in other lives and have completed their earth plane existence; they are now in the spirit world, assisting you with *your* life's journey.

However, some people view guides not as spiritual entities with consciousness outside of themselves, but as part of themselves. They feel that guides are their 'higher self' personified. Although they regard a guide as a way to access their intuition, they feel that their guide is actually a part of themselves that they are not normally in touch with. Psychologists usually share this view, explaining that guides are aspects of ourselves that we haven't yet 'owned' or integrated into our personalities.

I don't believe that these two points of view exclude each other. I don't believe there is anything 'out there' that isn't you, anyway. The spiritual beings are you, just as the sky and the sea and the stars are you. I believe that each person in our life, whether or not he or she has a physical body, represents an aspect of ourselves. In a larger sense, each person in my life is a part of me. Whatever the reality, many past life therapists find it enormously valuable to work with guides – they report that it is much easier to connect with past lives if they first connect their patient with his or her guide. I have heard this view consistently from past life therapists around the world.

✳

WHAT DO GUIDES DO?

Guides are spirit beings who are just as interested in us as we are in them. When you have a problem, and suddenly a solution seems to come out of nowhere, that is often the mark of a guide's intervention. Moments of inspiration can be the result of a guide's assistance. Those times when you are feeling down and then suddenly feel uplifted (again, for no apparent reason) can also indicate a guide's intercession. Guides can assist creativity, abundance and healing and can help harmonize difficult relationships. They also can help you with cultivating personal qualities such as forgiveness, acceptance and love. They can be your protectors and help you avoid dangerous situations. Guides can even help with more mundane issues such as getting parking spaces, finding lost property or choosing the right dress when you are shopping. And you can use a guide to connect with your past lives.

In addition to assisting the past life recall processes, one of the primary reasons for guide contact is to allow us to understand that there are dimensions beyond our physical, earthly existence. Guides give a more expansive view beyond our humanity and can be a source of spiritual inspiration.

Not so commonly known, however, is that in return for these gifts from the other side we offer a great deal to these guides. Just as we are evolving and growing by working with the challenges that life has to offer, so our guides too are evolving. They do so through working with us. You don't stop evolving once you die, and guides are evolving in the same way that we are.

*

INFORMATION FROM GUIDES

Metaphysical tradition holds the belief that if a spirit says something, it must be true. I would like to state that just because someone dies, he doesn't automatically become the sage on the mountain. If he was a couch potato when he was alive, he will most certainly be a couch potato when he is dead.

There are entities on the other side that are desperate to communicate and they will chatter endlessly, whether or not their information is worthwhile or even accurate. There are entities that are no wiser or clearer than any of your neighbours. For example, although you might value the opinion of your neighbour, you wouldn't necessarily drop everything and move to Tahiti if she told you to. When a guide gives you advice it is quite all right to question it and even reject it. Guides are like friends, and it is important to realize that both categories have opinions and personality quirks. These discarnate beings don't even necessarily agree with each other. If you compare the testimony of different guides channelled through mediums, for example, you will find that they very rarely agree.

Test any information against your own inner knowing. If it is useful, then take it as your own. If not, let it go. The important thing to remember is that *you* are making the choice – it is *your* decision. And ultimately *you* are responsible for the outcome of all the choices that you make.

Guides are effective sources of advice; however, it is easy to become too dependent upon them, to fall into the trap of continually asking their advice on every aspect of your life. Valuable though guides are, it is an important part of your evolution to be able to step beyond them and rely upon your own inner knowing. When you do this, you are connecting with your higher self – that part of you that continues after the body is sloughed off. Your higher self is your direct connection to Spirit or God.

✳

TYPES OF GUIDES

There are many kinds of guides. Remember that like attracts like, so your guides will always reflect an aspect of yourself – though this is not always obvious. I know of one instance where a tough woman who taught self-defence was surprised to find that her guide was very soft and feminine. She was expecting a Viking or at least a Samurai warrior. Then she realized that her guide came to offer balance in her life. In the same way, someone who is very disorganized and flamboyant may get a librarian-type guide – again, to offer balance.

Guides can be fairies as well. Even angels can be guides. Although they are excellent conveyors of universal love, they are not always equipped to deal with earthly problems. People who come from cultures that honour the spirits of ancestors will often be presented with ancestors as guides.

Remember, it is not the form that the guide takes, nor the manner of communication, that is important. The importance lies in the value of the information to you. Once you have established a relationship with your guides, you might notice a distinct feeling when they are about. Sometimes it is like a tingling sensation in a certain part of the body: Ann's little finger, for instance, tingles when her guide is present. Rachel's body will sway to and fro as a 'yes' answer from her guide, and side to side if her guide is saying 'no'. Some people will hear their own name spoken, or be aware of a distinctive smell when the guide is close at hand. One man's guide came from a past life in a German country – whenever he came, he was accompanied by a distinct smell of sauerkraut. I get a tingling feeling between my shoulder blades when my master guide has something to say. Some people hear their guide speak, others get distinct visual images, and yet others just get a sense of what their guide is trying to communicate. The important thing is to begin to develop trust that will allow you to be aware of the communications that you are being given.

*

MASTER GUIDE OR LIFETIME GUIDE

I have attended numerous births, and there is usually a point at which an influx of energy can be felt. This can be the influence of the birthing guides that are in attendance, but more often it represents the arrival of the master guide. This is a guide who sometimes will stay with you for an entire lifetime. However, if there is a change in life direction or emphasis, the master guide will step back and other guides will come forward.

Often children report having an invisible friend. I believe that this unseen, imaginary friend is a child's guide – frequently the master guide assuming an identity with which the child can communicate as he develops. It's important to allow your child to have that guide, and not to discourage him or her or to deny the existence of the relationship. Especially in early childhood, the master guide is there as an ally or godparent watching over, protecting and loving the child.

When I was a child, every night just before bed I was aware that there was someone with me. I could never see this individual, but I could feel a wonderful, loving presence near me. This didn't seem unusual to me – it was as natural as breathing. It was like gravity: we never think about gravity, but it is always there. As I got older, the loving presence began to visit me less and less. I feel that being was my master guide, watching over me and protecting me during the night.

*

SPECIAL PURPOSE GUIDES

Although some guides are lifelong companions, other guides will come and work with you in one particular area. For example, in my healing work a Native American guide comes and assists me only while I am actually working with an individual. I have another guide who helps me with questions about diet. Very often an artist or musician will have a guide who helps with creativity.

A speciality guide may help you develop a particular quality, such as patience or perseverance or abundance. I have a speciality guide who helps me just with my dreams – to program, remember and understand them – and another who assists me with past life awareness. There can even be speciality guides who can help you with something as ordinary as shopping. I have a wonderful, voluptuous, red-headed shopping guide who has yards of dangling bracelets up her arm, is dressed outrageously from head to foot and who speaks with a thick accent. When I'm at my wit's end shopping and can't seem to find what I need, she'll come right in and . . . hey presto! Straightaway I find the perfect item.

*

SHORT-TERM GUIDES

Sometimes a guide will arrive for just a short period of time. For example, I was in New Mexico doing some healing work with a man who had just been in a traumatic motor accident. Just as I was about to begin, an old Pueblo Indian woman guide came through and gave me unusual but specific information on how to work with my patient. I have never seen this guide before, and have never seen her since. But I took her advice – with excellent results.

Later that day I spent some time with Dancing Feather. I asked him about the advice that had been given, because it was so unusual. He said that the information given was very accurate according to Native American ways. (Now deceased, Dancing Feather occasionally comes to me as a guide, and often appears to those who attend my seminars.)

Sometimes these guides, such as the old Indian woman, appear only in a particular location. Once I was attending a festival in a coastal village in Madeira, off the coast of Morocco. We were enjoying the warm evening as we strolled along the sea wall. Suddenly a terrified, shawl-clad woman appeared holding an unconscious child. The child had fallen head first from the sea wall and was hardly breathing. The nearest doctor was hours away. As the frightened mother looked to us to help, I called for guide assistance. A guide, adorned in the vestments of a Catholic priest, appeared and within minutes the child was conscious and playing. This guide was never seen again – he was indigenous to that area.

If you are interested in accessing your past lives, short-term guides may appear or come at your request to help you. They will often present themselves during your dreams. Guides also come in for a short period during an emotionally or physically traumatic time.

*

PAST LIFE GUIDES

Usually your guides are those with whom you have shared a past life. A guide may be someone who taught you or gave you guidance, or someone for whom you felt a deep love. These guides will often occur in a form that would be familiar to you from the past life that you shared. For instance, if you had a past life in the south of France in a convent in the seventeenth century, you might find that your guide was the abbess and dresses accordingly.

I was very intrigued with a phenomenon that spontaneously occurred again and again when I began doing past life regressions with my clients. A guardian figure would appear in the inner explorations. Sometimes the guardian or guide would appear in period clothes. Sometimes it would come as a light or sound or symbol, and sometimes even as an animal. But there was always a wonderful, loving, guiding feeling that accompanied these guides.

There seems to be something inherent in our inner journeys that allows guardian beings from past lives to surface. Not only do they spontaneously appear for people who are being regressed, but they also appear in other inner voyages. People who have had near death experiences often report that they were guided by very protective, loving spiritual entities. Meditators and even individuals who spend time in isolation tanks report 'seeing' guides and guardians from the past. Perhaps it is when we take the time to be still and turn our awareness inwards that their presence can be felt.

*

PRESENT LIFE GUIDES

At times your guide may be someone whom you have known in this life but who has since died. Often this will be a deceased grandparent or someone whom you cared for as a child. Very often in my regression work we discover that an individual's guide is someone whom they had been very close to in the present life but who is now deceased. There is an emotional connection between the two that goes beyond time and space. Although the essence of the deceased guide stays the same, sometimes their personality changes when they are in the spirit world. My Cherokee grandmother was very stoic and quiet when she was alive; she carried herself with the dignified demeanour of an Indian elder and was reserved with all her grandchildren. Although I respected her, she wasn't the kind of grandmother whom you wanted to cuddle. I was therefore surprised when, one day many years after her death, she appeared in my dreams to give me guidance from the spirit world. Gone was the stern gaze, and in its place was a wondrous, glowing Indian face filled with warmth, peace, quietness and grace. I continue to feel her presence from time to time both in my dreams and in my waking life.

A guide can even be someone who is still alive. The very first time I attempted to contact a guide, I 'saw' a statuesque woman in her fifties who radiated magnificence. Two weeks later I went for my first Rolfing session – a type of massage. When the door swung open, I was astonished to be greeted by the exact image of the woman I had seen two weeks previously in my meditation. Over the next few months, as her sturdy fingers kneaded my body, this lovely woman graciously healed my body and soul. At that time in my life she was indeed a guide to me. Although she wasn't consciously aware of being my guide, nevertheless her higher self was my guide. With the exception of a guru, these living guides are not usually aware of the service that they are rendering. When you dream about someone you know in this life and, in the dream, he helps you in some way or acts out a part that is significant, often that person's higher self is actually assisting you and giving you guidance.

Guides are different from ghosts. A ghost is basically someone who has died and hasn't fully realized or accepted it. A ghost is still on the earth plane – without a body – and may be confused, sad or even angry. It's important to appreciate that ghosts cannot hurt you. When someone has had difficulty with a ghost they haven't been harmed by it but they have been shaken by their own fear. Ghosts are at a great disadvantage because they no longer have a body. The kindest thing to do if you encounter a ghost is to talk to him or her as you would anyone who is confused or unhappy. Let him know that he should go to the Light. Be gentle but firm.

*

SPIRIT ANIMAL GUIDE

Spirit emissaries can appear in many forms. Native cultures' use of totems (also called animal guides, power animals or spirit animals) is well documented. Members of these cultures believe that each person has an animal spirit or a power animal that can give assistance and strength – it is personal 'medicine'. There can be one animal or more assisting at any point in time, although usually there is one major totem that is influencing, guiding and teaching.

Animal totems function as spirit guides for those in native cultures, and they often appear in meditations and past life regressions as guides for those who have had past lives in native cultures. However, anyone from any culture can benefit from accessing their totem animal.

Each spirit animal has different qualities or abilities. By communing with one particular totem you gain access to its qualities. Although some cultures assign different meanings to particular power animals, there are some similarities. Often a person with the bear totem will be a good healer and have the introspection of bear, but will be challenged to come out of the cave. Someone with a deer totem may be involved with people, inter-relating with others, and may be very fertile in life. They may also have a gentle nature like deer and sometimes need protection for themselves from hunters, as some people may prey on them. People with the eagle totem often see into other dimensions and have ESP abilities, yet often find themselves alone.

There are a number of ways in which you can find your power animal. It may come to you repeatedly in a dream or meditation. Alternatively you may recognize you animal totem by observing which land or sea creatures you are drawn to. Sometimes a personal totem may be your favourite animal since childhood. A power animal may come to you in unusual ways: for example, if an owl's feather drops at your fcct as you walk in the woods there is a good change that the owl is one of your totems. If you feel particularly drawn to a painting that features horses, and then someone sends you a photograph of a horse, and then horses start to appear in your dreams, and over and over horses in one form or another appear in your life, there is a good chance that the horse is your totem.

Observing the attributes of particular animals is also helpful to discovering your totem. For example, bears wake up slowly in the morning and tend to be creatures of habit, travelling the same path each day. If you leap out of bed in the morning full of energy to start your day and tend to vary your activities it is unlikely that the bear is your totem. Finding out the attributes of various animals and comparing them with your own personality can be helpful in finding your totems. Your power animal can bring an understanding of what strengths you have as well as assisting you in times of distress. You can communicate with your totem animal in a similar way to that in which you communicate with a guide that takes a human form.

As we move into a time period where a planetary consciousness is focused on contributing to the healing and understanding of the earth, the value of animal totems will increase. Accessing with your animal totem, even if you haven't had past lives in native cultures, will help you unite with the earth. This is healing for all.

I have included a meditation to assist you in connecting with your spirit animal guide. You can read this meditation into a tape recorder to play back to yourself just before you go to sleep. Or you can do it with a friend and read the meditation to each other.

✳

ANIMAL GUIDE MEDITATION

Start by relaxing. When you are deeply relaxed you can connect with your guides and spirit helpers and totems. Just sit or lie comfortably in a quiet place and become aware of your own breathing. Stop for a moment and monitor the shallowness or deepness of your breath. Then take a really full deep breath in and fill your abdomen so that it expands just like a balloon. Keep holding your breath, longer and longer ... hold ... hold ... and then just let it out very slowly, easily and gently ... Repeat this exercise. Fill up your abdomen and allow it to expand ... hold that breath ... hold ... hold and then release ... let it go. Now take two shallow breaths, and feel the difference in your body between breathing deeply and breathing shallowly. Then allow your breath to flow in a natural, effortless way for a few moments. . . . Good.

Next focus your attention again on the area of your abdomen. With each breath feel yourself expanding and contracting. Really feel the air entering you, and feel your body expand. As your breathing becomes more rhythmical, turn your attention to the oxygen entering through your mouth and nostrils. Visualize yourself breathing in the purest, cleanest and healthiest air. Give this air a colour, and see that colour radiating down deep inside the cavity of the lungs, oxygenating and revitalizing all the parts that it reaches. Imagine that the oxygen you are breathing is healing and regenerating your lungs and your entire circulatory system ... aaah, that feels so good!

Now allow yourself to slip down to an even deeper level of relaxation. Keep your attention on your breathing. Another deep breath ... hold it, and then exhale. Let it go slowly and let out a gentle sigh ... mmmmm ... that feels so relaxing and calming. Your body is feeling rested; all cares and tensions are just fading away.

Next time you breathe in, put your consciousness down into your legs. Visualize your legs like empty vessels, and now fill those vessels with breath. See and feel the whole area around your legs being filled with a pure, cleansing breath. As you slowly exhale, feel your legs become heavier and heavier ... sinking into the floor beneath you, they feel incredibly relaxed and the muscles become more and more free of tension. Your deep breaths allow your body to relax with freedom and ease.

Take another long, deep breath and fill your hips and buttocks. As you exhale, feel those powerful muscles relaxing and letting go. Good. Now move your awareness up the body and breathe into your entire torso area, filling your lungs and back and chest and shoulders with breath. Hold. ... Hold. ... Hold ... and now exhale completely. Good. Your entire torso is now completely relaxed.

As if you were filling up a long balloon, breathe into your right arm. When you exhale, feel your arm relax and let go. Feel it becoming very, very relaxed and heavy. Now breathe into your left arm and let go. Good. Now breath into your neck and head. Fill your entire neck and head with breath, and when you exhale let all thoughts, cares and concerns just drift away. Just drift away. Good. Now your entire body is relaxed and feeling good. Continue with nice, full, easy breaths. Be conscious of the oxygen filling your lungs and being released from your lungs. In and out. In and out. There is a rhythm and cadence to the universe. At this moment your breath is aligning with that rhythm and cadence. You are breathing in harmony with all the patterns and rhythms of life. Really feel and imagine and be aware of this. You have a short time to do so.

Now that you are completely relaxed, you can begin an inward journey which will assist you in finding your animal spirit guide. In your imagination, travel to a beautiful place in nature. You can imagine some place that you have been before where you felt very comfortable and good, or you can travel to a place that exists in your imagination. Not everyone is a visual person, so if you have difficulty visualizing this beautiful location just get the feeling of it. Feel how good it would be to find yourself in this lovely place. Get a sense of the freshness of the air and the strength of the earth beneath you. Take just a moment really to imagine yourself in this beautiful place in nature. (If you are making a tape, you might leave some space here.) Imagine as you are in this place in nature that you are feeling very healthy and well. Good. Now find some place to sit down – it might be on a boulder or a tree stump or a sand dune – and make yourself comfortable.

As you are sitting, imagine that a mist is beginning to form. The mist becomes thicker and thicker until you cannot see anything around you. As you sit in this mist your inner intuition – your sixth sense – is expanding. Although you cannot see anything, you can feel the approach of your totem animal. You can feel the strength and the wildness and the power of your totem. Closer and closer. Reach out now into the mists and touch your spirit animal helper. Do you seem to be touching fur, feathers, reptilian scales or something wet like a creature from the sea? At the moment of your touch there is instant rapport between you and your totem animal. As the mists clear, you can see or feel the presence of your guide. You have a few moments to commune with your guide, who may 'speak' to you or just be with you in silence and in love.

When you are complete, say goodbye to your animal guide. Know that you can be together again and again in the silence of meditation.

✳

ANGELS

History and mythology are full of references to angels. They have inspired artists and writers as well as religious leaders. Beyond the myth, angels are real. They carry the essence of innocence and purity, and are touched by the hand of God. They are messengers from Spirit. Angels are associated with higher nature, beauty, peace, joy, fulfilment, laughter and love. They are here to help us heal lost faith, broken trust and innocence, and to lay down the burden of fear, uncertainty, guilt, pain and worry. They help to replace feelings of unworthiness and insecurity with joy and belonging. Angels assist us in touching a powerful yet gentle force which encourages us to live life to the fullest. They enable us to live with joy instead of with fear. Angels help us to enter the world of love.

They are different from guides in that they have not lived an earth-time existence: angels are of the stars and guides are of the earth. Divine beings who have not experienced the earth plane in a human body, angels do not have karma or evolutionary issues to work out from time on earth. Angels are celestial beings and are of a higher vibrational level than guides. Angels are the essence of purity.

There are many different types of angels, from nature angels to angel messengers to your very own guardian angel, and they can each serve different functions in your life. A nature angel is a guardian or protector of a particular area such as a mountain; the entire mountain will be under the care and guardianship of one angel. Or a lake can have an angel that watches over it. Different places in nature that have a special feeling are most often under the protective kindness of an angel. There are archangels such as the Archangel Michael with his sword of truth that serves as a guardian for our entire planet. And there are messenger angels that will sometimes take on human form for brief periods to send a message, to offer help in time of danger or teach an important lesson.

In my travels, people have shared with me remarkable stories about angels both with and without wings; each story carries with it a magical feeling of light and love. One woman, flying home from holiday, decided to finish her last roll of film by taking pictures of some clouds through the plane window. A few days later she received an urgent phone call from the film processors, who asked her to come down to the shop. When she arrived they wanted to know how she had produced the images on her cloud pictures. 'What images?' she said. 'They are just clouds!' Then they showed her the photos. In the middle of her cloud pictures was the most beautiful angel with large golden wings and a radiant smile. She said the angel looked male, with short brown hair, and was in very clear detail. One man told me that as a young man he had lived in the country, and on his family's land was a small lake. One day he took a walk by the lake and saw two angels flying back and forth over it. He ran to get his brother, who was eighteen at the time. He said his brother didn't want to come, but he dragged him, and when they got to the lake the angels were still flying back and forth, apparently not noticing him or his brother. The man said that to this day his brother won't talk about 'the angel incident'. Both these stories might be examples of nature angels.

Another man told me how he broke down on a narrow mountain road during a winter blizzard. A part of his four-wheel drive truck was broken, and he was miles away from any assistance. He had just about given up hope when a man came along in a truck who just *happened* to have the part that he needed, and helped him pull his truck out of the snow where it had got stuck. My informant said that, when he turned to thank the man after he got his truck started, not only were the helpful stranger and his vehicle gone but there were no tyre marks in the snow! These amazing stories are just a few among many that are related to me during my travels and at my seminars. I have no way of verifying them, but the sheer volume of stories involving angels or angelic intervention gives some credence to the idea that angels are real and are here to help us.

The guardian angel is a very special kind of angel. This kind of angel is with you from the time of birth and can help you to explore the special gifts that you were born with; it will also help you to find ways of freely expressing your gifts. An angel's main purpose is the focused transformation of human attitude, always moving it towards the light.

Angels appear in many different forms. Though it seems to be a rare occurrence, the form that most people associate with angels is the traditional church window angel with wings. Almost every culture throughout the world has adherents of winged angels. Native Americans called them the Bird People, alluding to their winged appearance. On my mantelpiece I have a carved wooden winged angel from Bali, looking like a winged mermaid. There are accounts of winged angels in ancient Mesopotamia and Assyria. There are angels in Christianity, Buddhism, Taoism, Judaic lore, Islamic tradition and in Zoroastrianism. The Vikings called them *valkyries*, the ancient Persians called them *fereshta* and the Greeks called them *horae*.

Some New Age adherents say that they are not actually wings but very fast energy emanations that we perceive as wings. Nevertheless there are reports of these divine winged creatures all over the world.

More common are reports of angels appearing in human form. These angels appear when they are needed and then sometimes mysteriously disappear. They seem to take a form that is comforting and pleasing to the individual to which they appear. I have heard numcrous reports of the physical appearance of these angelic beings. They appear as both male and female, both young and old, all different races, some well-dressed, some shabbily dressed. They all seem to offer guidance and help in a non-intrusive way.

There is another way that the angelic realm affects humanity and that is when an angelic energy superimposes itself on someone. When this occurs a person may unwittingly offer assistance and guidance to someone else in need . . . *and sometimes never even remember it!* It will seem that some tremendous force of goodness takes over momentarily and offers just the right message to another. Of course there can be many reasons for this but I like to think that one reason is angelic intervention.

Although some people have reported seeing angels, most angels aren't seen but felt. I have several different ways of telling if an angel is present. Often the wonderful smell of flowers accompanies their presence. Sometimes they announce their arrival with a slight breeze, even if all the windows are closed. This breeze is the flutter of wings (yes, some angels do have wings!). Sometimes you hear the sound of bells, chimes or trumpets when they come. I believe that the reason for the apparent sound of trumpets is that, when angels break into our dimension from theirs, the sound that most closely resembles that sound is trumpets. Sometimes someone will think they see a light, which can indicate the arrival of an angel. But the most usual way is that you feel there is an angel present. You will feel a warm wave of love wash over you. If you think you are in the presence of an angel, you most likely are.

From the archangels to your guardian angel, who is your personal comforter and friend, right now angels are bridging our physical reality with their pure spiritual energy. Like a leaf falling softly on the still pool of our consciousness, with ripples growing outward in ever larger concentric circles, will we recognize their presence. As we trust, they will pour their blessings on us. They are a doorway to the divine within. Angels have been waiting for us to be ready, and now is the time – the time has arrived for angels to manifest for humanity. I believe that multitudes of angels are going to be making their presence known in the years ahead as we heal old wounds from the past and step into the future. Expect a miracle!

*

CALLING A GUIDE BEFORE PAST LIFE EXPLORATION

Before embarking on any past life exploration, whether it is while you are awake or just before going to sleep, it is valuable to spend a few minutes requesting your guide or an angel. After you have spent a few minutes relaxing (you can use the guided process below), visualize your guide. If you don't have a visual image for your guide, then imagine or sense a large, glowing sphere of golden, white or silvery light. Feel yourself surrounded by a bubble of light and love and protection. After you have done this you might say to yourself, either out loud or quietly: 'Dear guardian, I ask for your assistance and guidance as I explore my past lives. Help me understand who I have been and why I have chosen those past lives. Help me to forgive and heal any blockages and barriers that have originated in the past. I ask for assistance to heal old wounds and old pain, even if I don't consciously remember my journey to the past. I send peace and give thanks for your loving blessings.' I have found that this invocation to help produces remarkable results. Remember: treat your guides and angels with love and respect, and give thanks for the blessings that are received.

✳

GUIDE MEDITATION

This meditation can be spoken aloud or taped to assist you in opening to your guides.

You are about to embark on an exciting journey to that inner place deep within yourself. Once you have tapped into this inner place, you will have access to an inner source of great strength, power and peace. You are commencing a journey where you will discover your sanctuary and encounter your master guide. To prepare for this journey across the bridge of time, lie or sit in a comfortable position with your spine straight and your arms and legs uncrossed.

Do this now . . . good.

As soon as you are perfectly comfortable, allow your eyes to close softly. Now inhale. Completely fill your lungs with air . . . hold for three seconds . . . and as you exhale, feel yourself relaxing.

Good. Now take another deep breath . . . even deeper than before . . . hold . . . and exhale completely. And, as you exhale, feel your entire body relaxing . . . completely relaxing.

Take one final deep breath and . . . without letting any air out . . . take in even more air and hold. And while you are holding that breath let your body relax. Really feel your body relaxing. Now let the air out. Let it all out . . . completely empty your lungs . . . all the way out . . . all the way out. . . . Relax. . . . And as you begin to breath naturally, notice as your stomach gently rises and falls . . . rises and falls . . . it's as though the entire universe were breathing through you. Just let all your cares and worries float away.

As these gentle, relaxing breaths continue, put your awareness in the middle of your chest. Your vital forces flow freely in and out of the middle of your chest. It's so peaceful to be so gently rocked by this natural rhythm. It feels so good to be aligned with your heart connection. There is no separation between you and that great force that surges through all of life.

Brilliant currents of vital life force energy flow in and out through your heart chakra with each inhalation and exhalation. When you breathe in you are drawing in shimmering, powerful, golden light . . . and when you exhale you radiate that light out to those you love and to the universe.

Your body is very relaxed. The small muscles around your eyes are utterly relaxed and smooth. Your brow is relaxed and tranquil. Your jaw muscles are very relaxed. Your thoughts dissolve and just fade away. An inner glow envelops you. You feel so fluid . . . so whole. Take a deep breath in and out. You feel so loved and lovable.

Again, one more deep breath in and out . . . let everything go . . . relax. . . . You are in complete harmony with all of life.

Now imagine a very beautiful place in nature. Perhaps it's somewhere that you've been before or somewhere that exists only in your imagination. Spend just a moment imagining this place as real, imaging as many specific details as possible. For example, if there are flowers in your sanctuary, smell and touch them. Use all your senses to experience this place in nature. Spend some time imagining or sensing that you are walking or running in this place . . . see yourself healthy and carefree. Imagine that you are breathing deeply of the fresh, clean, refreshing air. Somewhere in this place is a clear, still pool. Take a moment to imagine or sense it. It might be a pond with moonlit secrets hidden in its depths, or a spring-fed pool where you can see your own reflection – but altered, as if in a dream. Or perhaps it is a satin, glass-still lake.

As you stand near this still pool, you notice that a mist is forming near it. The spiralling mist begins to form a cloud that hugs the earth. From the centre of this cloud you are aware of a faint hum . . . a hum that gets louder and louder . . . a hum that seems to resonate with the very centre of your being. Intuitively, you are aware that your master guide is approaching. The very centre of this swirling mist is the arrival point for your master guide.

This guide has come forth through the ages to be with you, to guide you and offer you unconditional love and support. Through the mist, you can feel in every cell of your being the all-pervading love and absolute, unconditional acceptance given you by your guide. Your guide is coming forth from the ages to provide you with insight and guidance and love. This being knows you intimately and has been awaiting your call.

Now reach out your hand into the mists. As you do so, be aware and feel your guide's hand gently slipping into your own. In this moment allow yourself to feel a relaxation so deep that it touches the very core of your being. The mists are beginning to clear and you have the opportunity to meet your master guide. If you are not able to 'see' him or her, get a sense or 'feeling' of your guide.

Greet your guide. Ask your guide's name. Just accept whatever comes forth. Spend some time talking to your guide. Ask if he or she has any special advice for you. Or ask any questions that you might have. Or you may simply want to sit with your guide. You may do this now. Your guide can help you in your past life explorations or assist you during your dreams. Know that you can visit this place time and time again, and you can visit your guide whenever you want.

Say goodbye to your guide.

At this time you may like to drift off to sleep. If you want to return to normal waking consciousness, however, simply take a deep breath . . . and in your own time, when you are ready, allow your eyes to open gently.

After you have done this guide process, begin to remember and record your dreams (see Chapter 5). Watch for a loving being appearing again and again. Even if that being takes different forms in your dreams, the feeling emanating from it will be the same. Over time these recurring sensations and images will become a familiar indication of your guide's presence. Be alert to these sensations – otherwise at the start you may discount them. The more you open up to, believe in and interact with these guides, the stronger they become as an integral part of your life.

As you begin to connect with your guides and angels you'll find it much easier to recall past lives. This is because your guides contribute to a feeling of safety while you are exploring past lives both in your dreams as well as in regressions in waking life. I strongly recommend working with a guide in your past life explorations. I find in my own work that the best results in past life regression occur when an individual feels safe, and this always happens when one is connecting with their higher guidance. In fact, I find the attendance of a guide so helpful that I rarely do a past life regression now without calling upon their assistance. Their loving presence helps direct the course of the therapy.

8

*

Past Lives,
Future Lives

O ne foggy morning, as a small child, I sat forlornly on a
rusting swing. My feet barely reached the ground as I
shuffled my toes back and forth on the ground. Suddenly I
turned. I thought I sensed someone approaching, but no one
was there. I can remember a deep sense of calm and belonging
settle over me. I no longer felt alone.

This memory had faded into the deep recesses of my mind
and was completely forgotten until some thirty years later,
when I was endeavouring to go back in time to visit myself as a
small child. I popped out of my imagined time tunnel to find
myself comforting a very young me as she sat slumped on a
rusty swing. I told her I loved her unconditionally. I let her
know that she had some tough times ahead, but that she would
make it, and her future would be wonderful. As I talked to her,
she straightened up and a heavy weight seemed to be lifted
from her spirit.

Coming back into present time, I was astonished. Not only
had I travelled back and visited my younger self, but as a small
child I *remembered* the visit! I don't remember someone talking
to me that foggy morning but I remember feeling that someone
who cared for me was by my side and, even though I couldn't
see whoever it was, I knew that I didn't need to feel lonely any
more. It was a remarkable experience.

*

CHANGING THE PAST

I believe that not only the future but also the past is malleable! I have experienced profound changes within my own life and have observed changes within the lives of others simply by going back into the past (either in this life or in past lives) and altering it. You can actually alter the present through altering the past. Remarkably, when you change the present through changing the past, history is created to support the new present. There are many documented cases of individuals in therapy regressing to an earlier state of their life and healing wounds which occurred at that age. That healing then transforms their present-day lives. Past life therapy works in an even more extraordinary way. When you go back and release the trauma locked up in previous lifetimes, you can profoundly alter the history of your own existence right from the beginning. This sounds unbelievable, yet I have seen case after case where individuals in my seminars have literally gone back to the past, changed it, and come back to a changed present. The changes in the past seem to weave themselves through time, creating a new future. I believe that this is an idea whose time has come, and that you will find it appearing more and more often in films and books.

I discussed changing the past and creating a better outcome for yourself in Chapter 6. It is the most powerful method for resolution that I have personally ever worked with. No longer need you view yourself as a victim – you can take control of your life from Day 1. You have the power, you have the knowledge, so you can make it be the way it should have been!

However, if it seems too philosophical a concept to think about *really* changing the past ... then just think that you are changing the past that dwells within your mind. All the memories of the past, all the limiting beliefs and negative programming exist in your mind. Change your mind and change your life. Whether you believe that you are actually changing the past, or that you are just changing the past that dwells in your mind ... it works!

Jane came to my seminar on journeys into past lives. During one of the past life processes she worked on resolving the difficult relationship that she had with her mother in her present life. She felt that she had made excellent progress. In the process she had discovered and changed a traumatic past life that she had shared with her mother. The next day she 'coincidentally' got a call from 'her mother' – who explained that she was not Jane's mother but actually her grandmother! She went on to explain that Jane's real mother was the woman whom Jane had thought was her sister, and with whom Jane had an excellent relationship.

Most people would say that it was always this way and that Jane just found out. That, of course, is a very logical explanation and it makes sense. I believe that reality is created by 'agreement'. If many people 'agree' on something, then it becomes a 'reality'. For example, lots of people 'agree' that Picasso was a great painter. Thus Picasso is a great painter because people 'agree' on the value of his art. If no one had ever 'agreed' on this, then Picasso would not be a great painter.

I believe that 'form', too, coalesces around our collective 'beliefs' and 'agreements'. For example, the world used to be flat. At a certain time in our history, everyone would have agreed that the world was flat. All the evidence available at the time 'proved' that the world was flat. Now the world is round. All our scientific evidence 'proves' that the world is round – and it 'proves' that the world was *always* round. What if, in the future, it was proved that the earth is actually a hologram, projected from another universe? All the scientific evidence would 'prove' that the world was a hologram – and that it had always been a hologram.

I believe that we are constantly changing not just our 'present', but our 'past' and 'future' as well, from any given point in time. I believe that the universe is a pulsating, fluctuating ocean of consciousness with all time occurring simultaneously.

I believe that we are all intimately connected in this sea of consciousness. When you release an old blockage, not only does it help you but it is like a pebble dropped in a still pool whose ripples are felt at the farthest shore. Not only are your immediate family and friends positively affected by the 'ripples', but so is everyone else on the planet who shares your frequencies – even if they don't know you.

＊

THE RIPPLE EFFECT

Here is an example of how this ripple effect works. Daniel came to me because he was having problems with money. He would put time and effort into a project, but his financial gain would be disproportionately small. Daniel was very discouraged and felt that there must be some inner blockage causing the problem. He regressed to a life in the Middle East where he had been a merchant (he is of Middle Eastern descent in this life). In his past life he wasn't always fair in his business practices. In Daniel's regression he recalled a very traumatic event that was motivated by his past life business interactions.

It had been a searing hot day, permeating every corner and every fold of life. Though the darkness of the merchant's home had offered some respite from the heat, the lengthening shadows of the approaching evening were welcome. The merchant looked lovingly at his young son, who had just come in from outside.

Suddenly the merchant felt a presence in the doorway. He looked up. Menacingly filling the doorway, a man towered over him. It was a man whom the merchant knew only slightly. In an instant, however, the merchant understood why the man was there. The merchant had recently unfairly got the better of him in a business transaction.

Seemingly in slow motion, the man in the doorway raised a dagger high above his head. He rushed forward. In one silken movement he slit the throat of the merchant's son . . . and then ran out.

The scene was so traumatic that Daniel came out of his regression. I said, 'As painful as it seems, you can go back into that scene and change it. Doing this will have a positive and powerful effect on your present life.'

Reluctantly Daniel went back into his past life memories. He replayed the scene until the man in the doorway held the knife high overhead. He then changed the scene and imagined the man dropping the knife and running away. I said: 'Go forward in your life as a merchant.' He then 'saw' himself treating people very fairly. His reputation as a man of honour spread throughout the land. He 'saw' himself growing old and becoming more prosperous with each passing year. He 'saw' his son growing up to become a fine young man and an honourable merchant like his father.

As a result of exploring and changing his past life memories, two things occurred. Immediately Daniel's business began to turn round and now he is a very prosperous businessman. The second event that occurred was extraordinary. In Daniel's regression he saw that his teenage son in his present life was also the son who was killed by having his throat slit in his Middle Eastern life. His present life son had had a constant sore throat from the time that he was a small boy (most likely unresolved trauma from having died from a slit throat). But from the moment when Daniel changed his past life his son's sore throat went away, and has not returned although some eight years have passed. This is particularly interesting because Daniel had never told his family about the regression, because he thought they wouldn't understand about that kind of therapy.

In other words, Daniel changed the past and released an old blockage, and it had a ripple effect on those around him – even though they didn't know what he had done. Not only does this ripple effect influence those immediately around you, but the ripples spread through the universe to affect everyone else on the same frequency. It could be that, after Daniel's regression, halfway around the world there was another individual who was struggling with money problems. The next morning she could have got up feeling that a heavy burden had been lifted, although she didn't know why. We are connected. When one is uplifted we are all uplifted.

I'm often asked if, when we change the past, we can make a mistake that could influence others in a negative way. I have never seen this occur. I believe that there is a guiding force in life which makes sure that, when you 'change the past' while you are regressed, it contributes only good for everyone.

I find this guiding force at work in my affirmation meditations. There are times when I have affirmed for something and it almost instantly appeared. There have been times when I have affirmed for something with my whole heart and nothing happened. Usually, when my affirmations haven't been successful, just around the next bend in my life a wonderful opportunity opens for me that my affirmation would have precluded. I believe the reason for this is that loving guiding forces are always at play in our lives. So please do not be concerned that, if you change the past, it might have devastating effects on the whole world. Someone is guiding you and your process for the highest good of all concerned.

*

FUTURE LIVES

Some people find it valuable to visit their future lives or to have their future self come back through time and space to give advice and guidance based on what they gained in the future. I often do a 'future life' process in my seminars, and many people feel excited about what they discover. Because the time/space veil is thinning, it is becoming easier to travel in your meditations not only to the past but also to the future. Some people find that their inner confidence is renewed after they have viewed future triumphs. Others find that they can avert a difficult future by observing future possibilities and making present-day corrections.

It is possible both to travel into the future of your present life and to travel beyond this to lives into which you have not yet been born. The process is similar in both cases, and I have included below a meditation to get you started. However, before you start I would like to share some information that people often ask me for in my seminars.

Sometimes, people are concerned about how they will cope if

they see something truly terrible in their future, or in the future of someone they love. The future is as malleable as the past, and what you will be seeing is a future probability. The fortunate thing is that you are in a position to alter that probability! Whereas if you never saw what might come to be, you wouldn't realize what steps you could take to make things turn out the way you would like them to be.

You can reach future lives in a similar way to reaching past lives. First allow yourself to become very relaxed. You might deepen your breath or imagine a favourite place in nature. Perhaps imagine yourself sitting against a willow tree as you listen to a bubbling stream nearby. Allow your entire body to become very relaxed, placing awareness on every part of your body. Let every part of your body relax as you fill each and every part with tranquillity. Know that every breath is allowing you to become more relaxed. You might imagine your guide is nearby. You have nothing to fear. You are at peace with the universe. You are surrounded by infinite love.

You might imagine that you are surrounded in a protective bubble of white light. You are very safe and protected. As you are sitting in nature, imagine that day turns to night. One by one the stars come out. The entire sky becomes filled with shimmering, luminous stars. One particular star takes your attention. As you watch, the star becomes brighter and brighter. It slowly begins to float down from the skies. It is moving towards you.

As it gets closer you can see that it is actually a spherical vehicle made of light and sound. It looks like a large, luminous bubble. You know this is a time machine.

As you step inside, you feel comforted by the lush, cocoon-like interior. Quietly, with only the softest hum, the vehicle lifts from the earth and begins to float gently. As you settle back into the soft cushions you can observe the entire canopy of stars overhead through the windows.

You feel your vehicle floating gently to earth again. As you step out of your time machine you find yourself by a beautiful, still pool. As you gaze into it you begin to have visions. You see a vision of who you are to become in a future life. Notice if you are male or female. Notice any people who look similar to your present-day friends or family. Scan your future life and note the area of greatest conflict. See if there is anything in your present life that you can do to avert this future possibility. Surround the entire scene with infinite love and return to your time machine. Begin to bring yourself to normal waking consciousness. You know that all that you have seen of your future was for your highest good, and you know that you are making any necessary adjustments in your present life to create an exciting, fulfilling future.

9

*

Time, Space
and Beyond:
The Next Step

I believe that our past, present and future lives are not
sequential but are all occurring at the same time. However,
because we are linear beings and because we experience our
lives in terms of 'past', 'present' and 'future', this book talks
about all of our lives as if they occur in a sequential manner. I
want now to address the issue of time in regard to past lives.
This is especially important, as I believe that our entire notion
and perception of time will soon be changing.

To help you understand this idea imagine a mirror ball hang-
ing above a ballroom and radiating reflections throughout it. As
the ball moves, the individual reflections move around the
room. Pick one reflection. Place your awareness on that single
reflection. Imagine that the particular reflection on which you
have focused is you and your current life.

You appear to be going 'forward'. The scenes around you are
changing as you seem to be going 'forward in time'. There are
other mirror ball reflections in front of you as well as behind
you. The reflections that are seemingly 'behind' you as you
move around the room are your past lives. They seem to be
'past' lives because they are seemingly 'behind' you. The reflections seemingly 'in front' of you are your 'future' lives. They
are seemingly 'moving through time' as well.

The distances between the reflections in front of you and the
reflections behind you seems to stay constant – perhaps two

feet between you and the closest reflection behind you, and three feet between you and the reflection in front. Given that you are in a perfectly spherical room, those distances will remain constant even though the mirror ball is moving. This gives credence to the illusion that time is completely staid, because, no matter where your reflection has travelled in the ballroom, there is always two feet between you and the nearest reflection 'behind' you and there is always three feet 'in front' between you and the nearest 'forward' reflection. This is measurable and constant.

Looking at this in terms of past lives and future lives, if one foot is equal to a hundred years, then it might seem that there are two hundred years between your current life and your past life and three hundred years between your present life and your future life. However, as you move up the beam of light towards the mirror ball (which is the source of your reflection), then the distances between you and the closest light beams in 'front of' and 'behind' you change, and the distances become much closer. This metaphor demonstrates how the separations between past, present and future are diminishing. The more we collectively move towards our Source, the more the perceptions of time and space will begin to change. The closer you move to the Source, the more diminished the boundaries between past, present and future will seem to be.

Here is another conceptual way to perceive the thinning of the boundaries of time. Imagine that, if you were to leave your individual mirror ball reflection and travel 'forward in time', eventually you would come full circle and reach your 'past' lives. Likewise if you travelled seemingly 'backwards in time', eventually you would come full circle and reach your 'future' lives.

All the reflections on the ballroom wall seem separate and individual. Some reflections seem like future lives, some like past lives, and some can be thought of as other people's lives. However, if you were to travel from your individual reflection to the Source, the mirror ball, you would see that all lives – past, present and future – all people and all matter are resonating from the same Source. We are not separate from anyone else. Neither are we separate from what we call the 'past' and the 'future'. All lives are coexisting, intertwined and dependent on each other right now.

Time is not an absolute. It is Infinite Eternity arbitrarily divided into portions called centuries, years, months, weeks, days, hours, seconds and so on. In the past we have thought of time as steady and non-changing. I believe that, the more you explore the inner universes within yourself, through meditation or spiritual practices, the more fluid time becomes. You can actually perceive time speeding up or slowing down. Time is a product of your perception. The only 'time' that actually exists is the 'time' that you are perceiving. When you are involved in something creative 'time flies by', and an hour seems but a short blink of an eye. By contrast, when you are waiting for a friend who is an hour late, time can seem to stretch for an eternity.

You can speed time up or slow time down subjectively. This is what I call entering 'hyper-time', an expression I coined because it most accurately describes this phenomenon. Webster's *New Collegiate Dictionary* defines 'hyper' as 'that which exists in a space of more than three dimensions'. Entering 'hyper-time' is literally stepping into 'time that dwells beyond the three dimensions'. In my Journey into Past Life seminars, I teach seminar participants how to enter 'hyper-time'. I use powerful breathing and movement techniques that I have developed to 'snap-shift' perceptual reality in order to enter into 'hyper-time'.

I have heard some remarkable stories from seminar participants who have integrated these techniques into their lives. One woman shared the following story with me. For eighteen years she had worked at the same job. To get there she always drove the same route, maintaining the same speed, and there was never any variation in traffic conditions. It had always taken her exactly forty-seven minutes to get from home to work. She told me that, after participating in one of my seminars, she decided while driving to work to use the techniques that I had taught. She entered 'hyper-time', but otherwise she did everything exactly the same as always. And yet she got to work in thirty-two minutes! This is not an unusual story. Many participants of my seminars have reported similar events in their lives.

Given the current laws that govern our physical world, it should be impossible to alter time in such a manner. But what if time really is fluid? Suppose time contracts and expands in a rhythmically pulsating universe? Suppose time is a function of our perception? Imagine that we can dramatically shift our perception and enter into a timeless source, from which emanates all beingness. Suppose we could travel to the dimensionless regions where time and space are born? Given these suppositions, we could in fact alter time. I believe that these suppositions *are* true. I believe we are each and every one of us both the perceiver and definer of 'time'.

The laws of quantum physics are expanding very quickly. I believe those changes reflect the pulsating waves of energy that are available to the planet right now. The past, the present and the future are melding into one another. Reality is not what it seemed to be for hundreds of years in Western culture. (Native cultures have had many more fluid, circular constructs for describing time than Western, Eurocentric cultures).

My near death experiences on the 'other side' led me on a quest for self-understanding and to find my way back 'home' again. I intuitively knew that there was a way to get back to the Light without dying. I knew there was a way to 'be home' and still exist in a physical body. I intuitively knew that there was a myriad of dimensions coexisting with the physical dimension, and that all we need to be aware of them is to tune an inner 'dial'. We don't need to die to get there. Just as right now there are numerous radio stations flooding your home or office, but you can't hear them unless you have your radio turned on and the dial tuned in, we need only to find our inner dial and to practise tuning in.

Most people think of the place that you go to when you die as 'heaven'. Instinctively we subconsciously think of heaven as somewhere way up above the clouds. But 'Heaven/Home' isn't up in the sky. It's here – now. It is a dimension coexisting within our physical reality. One way you know that you are close to that dimension is synchronicity – for example, when you think of something and it happens; you need something and it appears; you think of someone and they call. When I was in the Light, there was no time between thought and creation. My thoughts were instantly manifested. So one way to tell if you are tuning your 'inner dials' to 'home' is synchronicity. The closer you get to that dimension, the faster your thoughts become manifested in the physical world.

When I ponder the events of past lives, the prospect of future lives and the value of being Here Now, in a human body, it occurs to me that living life fully and passionately in present time is very important. I've noticed that when individuals release blockages from the past, both through dreams and through waking regressions, they experience an expansion of their life force energy – their passion. Most people assume passion to be of a sexual nature, but I believe that sexual passion and spiritual passion spring from the same source – the Source of All That Is. It occurs to me that perhaps passion isn't only an end result of past life therapy, but it is perhaps our passion for life that will allow us to heal the past and propel us into a glorious future.

There is nothing out there that isn't you. Because of the linear way that we perceive reality I don't think we can ever understand this intellectually, communicate about it verbally or even write about it in a comprehensive way. However, I do believe that deep inside each of us *we all do know this*. Deep inside, we have all experienced what this feeling is like. Even in the most fulfilled human being there is a longing, a yearning, and a remembering of that exquisite place of oneness and unity.

Each and every part of the universe is in actuality a part of you. You are the most astonishing blend of varied parts imaginable. We usually identify with our body and feel separate from all the other parts of ourselves. Sometimes we identify with our children or even our possessions (a man will run into a burning building to rescue valuables because in that moment he is identifying himself more with the valuables than with his body). But in fact you are living in a miraculous ocean of energy, and each part of that flow of energy is you. You might imagine all these parts as making up a gigantic orchestra. When there is a harmonization of all these parts, a vibration is created that resonates throughout the universe.

This is what my Native American ancestors mean when they talk about being in 'right relation' with all things. It means to honour and respect the livingness in all things. It means to honour the animal or plant that gives you life. It means to honour all life around you. It means to listen, *really listen*, and honour the reality of your neighbours. For they are not separate from you. They *are* you!

To be in 'right relation' with all things means living in harmony with all other parts of the collective spirit. One way to do this is to move to understanding and accepting unconditionally, without judgement, the reality of others. This also means moving towards accepting all parts of yourself as well, especially the parts that you have judged negatively. This includes accepting yourself and what you may have been in your past lives. Being in 'right relation' means helping others wherever you can without expectations or conditions, without expecting anything in return. It means acting with compassion and consciousness towards all other parts of that life force. This means that, no matter where you are and no matter what is around you, you should accept and honour the life force that is there. Know that there is no less life in your typewriter than in the beautiful apple tree that grows outside your window. Honour, accept and love the life that is all around you, for it is all you in different forms. Whatever you judge sets you further along the path of separateness. Whatever you love allows the orchestra of all your parts (which in its totality is God) to vibrate and sing with joy throughout the universe.

May Great Spirit that is both within you and all around you bless you in all that you do, so that all of your dreams in all of your lifetimes may manifest joy for all of us here, together forever in the magnificent, ever-expanding universe!

*
About the Author

*A*fter reading this book, you may want to meet Denise Linn in person. Denise regularly conducts seminars in almost every English speaking country in the world, as well as a number of non-English speaking countries, working through an interpreter.

For information about her seminars in the Northern Hemisphere contact:
New Life Designs
Arnica House
170 Campden Hill Road
London W8 7AS
UK
Tel: 0171–938 3788

In the Southern Hemisphere contact:
New Life Promotions
Lock Bag 19
Pyrmont
NSW 2009
Australia
Tel: 61–2–552–6833
Fax: 61–2–566 2354

For information about where to obtain Denise's Past Life Regression Tapes and Dream Programming Tapes contact:
QED Recording Services
Lancaster Road
New Barnet
Hertfordshire EN4 8AS
UK
Tel: 0181–441 7722

Piatkus Books

If you have enjoyed reading *Past Lives, Present Dreams*, you may be interested in other Mind, Body and Spirit books published by Piatkus. Titles include:

The Afterlife: An investigation into the mysteries of life after death Jenny Randles and Peter Hough
As I See It: A psychic's guide to developing your sensing and healing abilities Betty F. Balcombe
Awakening to Change: Your guide to personal empowerment in the new millennium Soozi Holbeche
Creating Abundance: How to bring wealth and fulfilment into your life Andrew Ferguson
The Energy Connection: Simple answers to life's important questions Betty F. Balcombe
Karma and Reincarnation: The key to spiritual evolution and enlightenment Dr Hiroshi Motoyama
Living Magically: A new vision of reality Gill Edwards
Many Lives, Many Masters: The true story of a prominent psychiatrist, his young patient and the past life therapy that changed both their lives Dr Brian L. Weiss
A Message of Love: A channelled guide to our future Ruth White
Pocketful of Dreams: The mysterious world of dreams revealed Denise Linn
Psycho-Regression Therapy: A system for healing and personal growth Dr Francesca Rossetti
Reincarnation Liz Hodgkinson
Stepping into the Magic: A new approach to everyday life Gill Edwards
Transformed by the Light: The powerful effect of near-death experiences on people's lives Dr Melvin Morse with Paul Perry
Yesterday's Children: The extraordinary search for my past-life family Jenny Cockell

For a free brochure with further information on our full range of titles, please write to:

Piatkus Books
Freepost 7 (WD4505)
London W1E 4EZ